The Spiritual Legacy

CELEBRATION FOR THE NATIONS AND BEYOND

Dr. Hana Ibberson, et al.

Scripture quotations [marked NIV] taken from the Holy Bible, New International Version Anglicised Copyright © 1979, 1984, 2011 Biblica. Used by permission of Hodder & Stoughton Ltd, an Hachette UK company. All rights reserved. 'NIV' is a registered trademark of Biblica UK trademark number 1448790

Scripture quotations are from the ESV® Bible (The Holy Bible, English Standard Version®), copyright © 2001 by Crossway, a publishing ministry of Good News Publishers. Used by permission.

Scripture quotations taken from the Amplified® Bible (AMP), Copyright © 2015 by The Lockman Foundation. Used by permission.

Scripture quotations from The Authorized (King James) Version. Rights in the Authorized Version in the United Kingdom are vested in the Crown. Reproduced by permission of the Crown's patentee, Cambridge University Press

Scriptures and additional materials quoted are from the Good News Bible © 1994 published by the British and Foreign Bible Society. Good News Bible © American Bible Society 1966, 1971, 1976, 1992. Used with permission.

All Scripture quotations are taken from *The Message*, copyright © 1993, 2002, 2018 by Eugene H. Peterson. Used by permission of NavPress. All rights reserved. Represented by Tyndale House Publishers.

Scripture quotations taken from the (NASB®) New American Standard Bible®, Copyright © 1960, 1971, 1977, 1995, 2020 by The Lockman Foundation. Used by permission. All rights reserved.

First Edition -2023

Copyright © 2023 Dr. Hana Ibberson
Cover Design Copyright © 2023 Deborah Ibberson
All rights reserved.

For permission or inquiry please email: hibberson@hotmail.co.uk

ISBN: 9798865930624

Also by Dr. Hana Ibberson

Shofar-blowing: Sounds From Heaven To Earth
1st edition (2021; Paperback, eBook)
2nd edition (2023; Hardcover)

In the book the author shows 'what shofar-blowing is all about' based on biblical references along with compiled useful information, practical guidelines, spiritual insights and historical encounters of shofar-blowing. It is a 'hands-on' material for shofar-blowing.

My Book For You, Friend
(2021; Hardcover)

The author tells you 'who you are' and guides you to the right way for your destiny. The book includes exciting stories to find your identity, to forgive others, to receive daily blessings, to avoid temptations and deliverance, and so on. Also, it contains the 30 day's journaling for a deeper relationship with God.

Post-Alpha: Follow-Up Guide
(2023; Paperback, eBook and Hardcover)

While being involved in the Alpha course over the years, the author has sensed a need for a follow-up after completion of the course and written a simple and practical book to take it all in and benefit from it. Especially, the book encourages attendees (guests) to help at the future Alpha which is not only a good way to build an Alpha team but also a great way to support the attendees (guests) in their faith journey.

To access and purchase any book of the author, simply visit to *Amazon* platform and type 'Hana Ibberson.'

DEDICATION

To the generation who will carry on the spiritual legacy

ACKNOWLEDGEMENTS

I sincerely wish to acknowledge indebtedness to the following contributors to this anthology by means of sharing and writing their own stories.

Gail Dixon

The author of *Beloved Warrior: Love is the weapon* and *Hidden Glory: Your Identity*

Colin and Mavis Harris

Joan Davies

The author of *Higher than mine: The memoirs of Joan Davies*

Jessie Ho

Sora Kim

Peter Ibberson

CONTENTS

PROLOGUE *1*

One
Legacy *3*

Two
Generation With No Experience Of War *12*

Three
Even If Noah, Daniel, And Job *28*

Four
Celebration For The Nations (CFTN) *45*

Gail's Story *47*

This Is My Story *51*

Colin And Mavis' Narrative *60*

Joan's Story *69*

Jessie's Story *73*

My Song Of Songs *77*

Our Talk On CFTN 2023 .... *90*

Five
Your Body Symphony For God *97*

Six

I Saw The Lord *108*

Seven

Why Jesus? *119*

Eight

Catch Me Up In Your Story, Lord *126*

EPILOGUE *153*

ABOUT THE AUTHOR *171*

PROLOGUE

The wisest but pessimistic man here on earth once said, 'what can a man gain from all his labour under the sun?' Generations come and generations go, but what remains forever? As he said, the earth remains forever. We are here today but won't be here tomorrow. Who will remember us after we will be gone? Perhaps no one remembers us later on but what we will pass on now to the next generation remains. Why?
It is history - His story!

I don't know the future but He holds it. I don't know what I'm passing on but He knows it. I don't know how long it remains but He controls it. I simply do what I can do now and surely He will do the rest. Why?
It is history - His story!

With long-term friendship among folks of *Celebration for the Nations* during the past years, here I begin a journey of leaving a valuable legacy for many spiritual sons and daughters now and to come. Please don't forget.
It is history - His story!

One

LEGACY

I sense that God is preparing the older generation like me to pass on a valuable legacy of our genuine faith in Jesus, *the messiah* to the generation to come for His next great and incomprehensible work.

Interestingly, according to the Cambridge Dictionary the secondary definition of 'legacy' is 'something that is a part of your history or that remains from an earlier time.' To be honest, how many of us can think seriously of the most valuable and long-lasting legacy, unlike its primary definition of money or property that we will receive from someone after death?

Well… here I am talking about a 'spiritual legacy' which is far more than a baton or a torch that we can pass on to the next generation to carry on. It is passing on the anointing, the blessing, and the call of God on us to our spiritual sons and daughters for the next level in spirituality. How does the legacy begin and then how will it be established? To make it short, it starts with our personal relationship with Jesus, *the messiah*. In other words, our stories started with Jesus in the past continue to our present faith journey with Him and then will be given to the future generation.

Have you ever thought that we are meant to be storytellers who pass down the epic of faith from one generation to the next? In the time of wilderness, the Israelites built a memorial of stones to tell their children about how the Lord had brought them out from slavery in Egypt and allowed them to pass through afflictions and many wars until they eventually entered into the Promised Land after crossing the River Jordan. Actually, making the memorial was God's idea as we see below. He knows exactly how easily we forget things unless we are continually reminded of them.

> When all the nation had finished passing over the Jordan, the Lord said to Joshua, 'Take twelve men from the people, from each tribe a man, and command them, saying, "Take twelve stones from here out of the midst of the Jordan, from the very place where the priests' feet stood firmly, and bring them over with you and lay them down in the place where you lodge tonight."' Then Joshua called the twelve men from the people of Israel, whom he had appointed, a man from each tribe. And Joshua said to them, 'Pass on before the ark of the Lord your God into the midst of the

Jordan, and take up each of you a stone upon his shoulder, according to the number of the tribes of the people of Israel, that this may be a sign among you. When your children ask in time to come, "*What do those stones mean to you?*" then you shall tell them that the waters of the Jordan were cut off before the ark of the covenant of the Lord. When it passed over the Jordan, the waters of the Jordan were cut off. So these stones shall be to the people of Israel *a memorial forever*' (*Italics mine*, Joshua 4:1-7; ESV).

Another example is found in the book of Esther. When Queen Esther and Mordecai instituted a joyous holiday, *the festival of Purim* after the saving of the Jews from a threatened massacre during the Persian period, it was for the remembrance of things past. Two days of the month were the days of deliverance from sorrow to joy and from mourning into a good day. Here is a summary of what and how it happened as the book of Esther describes (Esther 9:24-28; NIV):

> For Haman son of Hammedatha, the Agagite, the enemy of all the Jews, had plotted against the Jews to destroy them and had cast the *pur* (that is, the lot) for their ruin and destruction. But when the plot came to the king's attention, he issued written orders that the evil scheme Haman had devised against the Jews should come back onto his

own head, and that he and his sons should be impaled on poles. (Therefore these days were called Purim, from the word *pur*.) Because of everything written in this letter and because of what they had seen and what had happened to them, the Jews took it on themselves to establish the custom that they and their descendants and all who join them should without fail observe these two days every year, in the way prescribed and at the time appointed. These days should be remembered and observed in every generation by every family, and in every province and in every city. And these days of Purim should never fail to be celebrated by the Jews -nor should the memory of these days die out among their descendants.

Obviously, *the festival of Purim* was instituted for the memorial of Jewish deliverance in order to pass on to generation after generation. Every year *Purim* is celebrated on the 14th and 15th days of Adar, the twelfth month of the Jewish calendar.

By the way, when we see a war memorial, we are reminded of both a beautiful testimonial of the brave soldiers who died in battlefield and a tragedy of horrible war, aren't we? Generations come, generations go, but either good or sad stories of the war will pass on as long as the memorial remains.

Just mentioning the war memorial and the soldiers, I would like to share with you about my parents who experienced hard times during and after wars. Apparently, stories of a person who went through hard times never fail to encourage and inspire us. Like many others in war generations my parents started to accumulate their wealth from scratch. Of course, they were very hungry for many days, and poverty never seemed to be eradicated, or even reduced, until they tasted and saw God's blessings as they had truthfully obeyed His promises by faith whenever they faced challenges. For instance, one of the hardest things for them to do was to tithe their income when they barely survived for living from hand to mouth.

> Bring the full tithe into the storehouse,
> that there may be food in my house.
> And thereby put me to the test,
> says the Lord of hosts,
> if I will not open the windows
> of heaven for you and pour down for you
> a blessing until there is no more need.
>
> - Malachi 3:10; ESV -

Throughout the hard times my parents truly tested God's faithfulness and then grew strong in their faith. Now both of them are with the Lord in heaven; nevertheless, thankfully their spiritual legacy they had passed down to me is still with me now.

One of the distinctive attributes in my parents' legacy

is generosity. I have already mentioned about my mother's generosity in my book, *My Book For You, Friend*. Here I would rather tell you about my father's.

My father was extremely careful with money. When my siblings and I were younger, we held a grudge against him for that. Nonetheless, he was very generous with good works for God's sake. He was a bright man so even he was relatively old aged but studied hard to get a licence to practise medicine. Despite his wealth accumulated over the years, he didn't live in luxury but a simple life per se. I am not exaggerating to say that if you would bump into him on the street now, you wouldn't know whether he was rich or not. One day, out of the blue, I witnessed a remarkable and unforgetful incident which my father did to someone in the body of Christ.

A pastor who had begun a small gathering of people in the countryside came to see my father. He used to be a youth pastor at the church which my father was with but got kicked out of it due to his doctrine issue or, more likely, due to petty jealousy of the senior pastor. While he was praying concerning the church building for some time, the Holy Spirit prompted him to see my father. Yet, he really hesitated to do so. The more he resisted, the stronger the Holy Spirit urged him. At last, he surrendered to him, saying, 'Okay. I'm going now but won't ask him for a help unless he would offer me first.' The pastor stopped by my father to say hello. My father asked him about his family's living since he was miserably kicked out. He told him that God looked after his family mysteriously well since then. In the middle of their conversation, my father asked him whether he had a desire to construct a church building. The pastor simply mentioned about his plan without much expectation. To his surprise, my father told him that he willingly would help him in a building project if needed because he said that it was his long-held dream. Sometime later my father received a mail in which there was a beautiful church picture surrounded by peaceful country scenery.

As a matter of fact, I acknowledge that generosity is not simply an act but a character trait developed by God's grace in order to give away our resources to help the needy. We have learnt this from Jesus who first showed us the perfect example of giving away. It is very true that people whose many sins have been forgiven (by God) love to serve and to give away much as Jesus said (Luke 7:47).

Look at what the chief tax collector, Zacchaeus said to Jesus after encountering him, 'I give half of my possessions to the poor, and if I have cheated anybody out of anything, I will pay back four times the amount' (Luke 19:8; NIV). Generosity naturally flows out from the fountain of thankful and gracious hearts. Jesus came to the world to give his life (the highest and ultimate gift) as a ransom for many (Matthew 20:28). He gave the humanity all that he could offer: love, freedom, truth, authority, power, healing, his death, everlasting life, and His spirit.

So far I have just singled out one attribute (generosity) among many characteristics of true Jesus' followers and talked about it as an example. However, the closer we have an intimate relationship with God, the more we become a cheerful giver.

In fact, *Celebration For the Nations* (CFTN)[1] truly began with the immeasurable sacrifice accompanied by generous hearts, and then persistently carried on over the years. We will talk about it in great detail later on. It should be mentioned that in order to bring it forth, many gave away such precious sacrifices of time, prayers with tears, finance, sweaty labour, etc. Without all of these, there is no way for CFTN to take place over time. I would say that the sacrifice of the worshipper is the heart of CFTN which holds its true beauty. Let me close this chapter by quoting a beautiful story from the Bible.

> A Pharisee, Simon invited Jesus to dine with him at his house. An unnamed woman, known only as a 'sinner' in the city where she lived, came to Jesus with an alabaster jar of fragrant oil. She did a remarkable thing that no one ever thought of. She knelt behind Jesus at his feet and wept. And then she began to wash his feet with her tears, and wiped them with her hair. On top of it, she kissed his feet and anointed them with the fragrant oil.

What a shocking scene it was! The Pharisee was furious and criticised his honorable guest, Jesus for allowing her to conduct such things at his house. Yet, what she did for Jesus was out from her love and gratitude, therefore Jesus said,

---

[1] *Celebration* is interchangeably used for *Celebration For the Nations* (CFTN) throughout the book depending on the story tellers.

'… I tell you, her sins, which are many, are forgiven - for she loved much. But he who is forgiven little, loves little' (Luke 7:47; ESV) and

'Your sins are forgiven' (Luke 7:48; ESV).

In an act of love and gratitude her sins were totally wiped out, and she was saved by faith and released from her sins and had peace afterwards. I truly believe that this hits the DNA of CFTN: an act of worship with sacrificial love of the forgiven sinner.

Two

GENERATION WITH NO EXPERIENCE OF WAR

Being born and growing up in a Christian home are a great blessing in many ways. Children from a very young age can perceive and receive prayers, God's words, Christian virtues and godliness. As they grow, they can extend their knowledge of God. Religious beliefs and godly modeling of parents greatly influence the children during childhood.

On the contrary, I cannot deny that there is a danger of a love-hate relationship with the church and even God as the children grow in their understanding and faith. In a bad case, some children come to resent both the actions of the church and home. They perceive the church events as irresponsible and meaningless. Even they might feel that they have been misled and given a false sense of their position in Christ. If they get worse, they develop hostility towards the church and Christianity, especially during adolescence as they struggle with their own identity and their relationship with God.

While individuals begin to think about personal responsibility for their own commitments, life-styles and belief, adolescents or young adults cannot avoid tensions between the person they want to be and what others expect of them. If they would miss an opportunity to own the beliefs they could hold at this stage, their hearts would become cold and far from God. Thus, they come to a point of having a huge gap between the knowledge of God and the reality of God.

I myself had gone through that stage because I grew up in a godly Christian home. When I was very low and depressed due to my own failure during young adulthood, I bitterly resented God and even doubted His existence. 'How dare He fail me if He exists? My hope has gone.'

God is the Creator and thus has a unique and specific plan for each and every one. Does it surprise you if I would say that He often would fail us for that plan? He does it because He foresees it and knows that we cannot fulfill it without failure. 'Without failure, there is no success.'

A well-known name or characteristic for God is 'Jehovah-Jireh.' Its Hebrew meaning is 'the Lord will provide,' or 'God is my provider.'

> Abraham lifted up his eyes and looked,
> and behold, behind him was a ram,
> caught in a thicket by his horns.
> And Abraham went and took the ram and
> offered it up as a burnt offering
> instead of his son.
> So Abraham called the name of that place,
> 'The Lord will provide'; as it is said to this day,
> 'On the mount of the Lord it shall be provided.'
>
> - Genesis 22:13-14; ESV -

The ancient Hebrew word 'Jireh' (יראה) literally means 'to provide' or, more likely, 'to foresee.' As we can see in the occurrence of Abraham's faith test above, God had already seen the ram caught in a thicket whereas Abraham could not see it because of the intense stress and fear of his son's death ahead.

On a different note, from a viewpoint of etymology it is fascinating to understand how a word 'provide' is connected with 'foresee.' It is originally derived from Latin *providere*, meaning 'look ahead, prepare, supply, act with foresight': *pro* 'ahead' (from PIE root *per-* 'forward') + *videre* 'to see' (from PIE root *-weid* 'to see').

It does make sense that even God allows us to fail because He foresees a thing(s) which we cannot see now. Who knows perhaps we can fill the gap between the knowledge of God and the reality of God in that way? We can truly acknowledge His sovereignty over us as the Author of life by experiencing failures. Thankfully, my pursuit for 'knowing God' caused my life to turn around. Particularly, Proverbs 3:5-6 greatly challenged me, but on the other hand the scriptures promised me to guide for the future in the midst of my desperation. On a lighter note, I am not exaggerating when I say that every single card my husband and I received had the exact same scripture quoted in it on our wedding day. Has God reminded me of His sovereignty again as I began a new chapter of my married life?

> Trust in the Lord with all your heart,
> and do not lean on your own understanding.
> In all your ways acknowledge him,
> and he will make straight your paths.
>
> - Proverbs 3:5 and 6; ESV -

If you are the first believer in your family, what are you praying for now?

I witnessed a friend of mine from a different religion who was severely persecuted when she became a Christian. She cried to God when she was brutally beaten by her parents and then got kicked out of her house. Nevertheless, she became stronger in faith as she deepened her intimacy with God amid extreme persecution. This is what we can commonly find from many who are at risk for their faith in a society which people loathe Christians radically.

I also witnessed many who were severely sick and almost dying but were miraculously healed by prayers of Christians. Their faith becomes solidly strong and won't be shaken in any circumstances because of their divine encounter of Jesus. Their testimonies are truly powerful to influence others.

However, why it may not be true with the next generation of those precious people above? The reason is simple. The amazing and powerful testimonies are not theirs but either their parents' or grandparents.' In court, a second-hand account is often considered to be hearsay unless an exception to the hearsay rule applies. The second-hand witness would not be as powerful as a first-hand account because they have not experienced the happening(s) themselves in the first place.

In the same vein, our head knowledge of God is not the same as our experiential knowledge of Him until what we *know about* Him becomes what we experience and know Him personally. Let me illustrate this through an example. Let's say that you know 'falafel' but have never tasted it before. When you taste it, you truly know what it is. In case if you have no idea about 'falafel,' it is a common street food in Middle East as deep-fried spicy balls made from chickpeas or broad beans, served with a pita (a pocket bread) or wrapped in a flatbread. On this account, what we are told from either our parents or grandparents may not become real to us unless we have our own faith in God in the same way as they had.

We are well aware of the story of Exodus. The Israelites were set free from slavery in Egypt under the leadership of Moses after living there for 430 years as God said. 'Then the Lord said to him [Abraham], Know for certain that for four hundred years your descendants will be strangers in a country not their own and that they will be enslaved and mistreated there' (Genesis 15:13; NIV).

To brief the story, after the ten plaques in the land of Egypt, Pharaoh finally cast out all the Israelites when his firstborn son was killed. As Pharaoh and his army pursued after them, God used Moses to part the Red Sea [Reed Sea]. After all the Israelites crossed on dry ground, the sea closed down on the pursuing Egyptians and drowned them all.

During the time of wilderness God led the Israelites in the form of a pillar of cloud in the day and a pillar of fire at night. When they complained about water and food, God supernaturally provided for them. God fought for the Israelites when the Amalekites attacked them at Rephidim. When they arrived at Mount Sinai, God called Moses and His people to come up to the mountain and revealed Himself to them there. God then established the Ten Commandments and made the Mosaic covenant: if the Israelites would keep His Torah (laws) and in return He would give them the Promised Land.

After Moses died, God said to his successor Joshua, 'Moses my servant is dead. Now therefore arise, go over this Jordan, you and all this people, into the land that I am giving to them, to the people of Israel' (Joshua 1:2; ESV). As we see, God commissioned Joshua to take possession of the land and warned him to keep faith with the Mosaic covenant. The Israelites crossed the Jordan River to enter into the land and conquered it and then divided it among the tribes of Israel accordingly with the exception of the Transjordanian tribes - Reuben, Gad, and half of the tribe of Manasseh, the son of Joseph.

If God would make history with us, He would let us go through a wilderness period in our life in order to teach us (and the next generation). 'Where is the Lord...who led us through the barren wilderness, through a land of deserts and ravines, a land of drought and utter darkness, a land where no one travels and no one lives' (Jeremiah 2:6; NIV). 'History repeats itself.' Why? We with a sinful nature make the same mistakes which our forefathers did and go to the same path where they went unless we learn what God wants us to be and what to do.

From the story of Exodus, a couple of things should be mentioned before getting to the main points of this chapter. First of all, God took the Israelites the long way to the Promised Land rather than the direct route which would have taken only a few weeks.

> ... when Pharaoh let the people go, God did not lead them by way of the land of the Philistines, even though it was nearer; for God said, 'The people might change their minds when they see war [that is, that there will be war], and return to

Egypt. But God led the people around by the way of the wilderness toward the Red Sea; the sons of Israel went up in battle array (orderly ranks, marching formation) out of the land of Egypt.

- Exodus 13:17-18; Amplified Bible -

The direct route meant that the Israelites would go right past Egyptian fortresses, and God also knew that they were not ready for war. Obviously, they used to be salves not well-trained soldiers who knew 'how to fight.'

Secondly, God was displeased with all those who left Egypt but did not believe, saying that they (every person that is 20 years and older) would surely die in the wilderness except Caleb and Joshua. Both Joshua and Caleb were chosen with ten other men to spy the Promised Land and gave a positive report to Moses and the congregation of Israelites whereas the other ten discouraged them after 40 days of exploration.

Surely none of the men who came up out of Egypt, from twenty years old and upward, shall see the land that I swore to give to Abraham, to Isaac, and to Jacob, because they have not wholly followed me, none except Caleb the son of Jephunneh the Kenizzite and Joshua the son of Nun, for they have wholly followed the Lord.

- Numbers 32:11-12; ESV -

What can we learn from the story of Exodus? Here are the main points of the chapter. God reminds us that only those (even a few in number) who faithfully trust in him can inherit His promised land. 'For many are called, but few are chosen.'

Also, God is looking for those who can fight with unshakable faith in God like what Joshua and Caleb did. Apparently, it shows that only those who faithfully trust God and can fight God's war become heroic history makers.

Caleb quieted the people before Moses and said,
'Let us go up at once and occupy it,
for we are well able to overcome it.'

- Numbers 13:30; ESV -

So Moses said to Joshua, Choose for us men,
and go out and fight with Amalek.
Tomorrow I will stand on the top of the hill
with the staff of God in my hand.
So Joshua did as Moses told him, and fought with
Amalek, while Moses, Aaron, and Hur went up
to the top of the hill.

- Exodus 17: 9-10; ESV -

Joshua is a fascinating character to look at closely. He was born in Egypt prior to Exodus; hence he also had an experience of slavery. He was the son of Nun, of the tribe of Ephraim. His Hebrew name was originally Hoshea (הושע meaning 'save'), but Moses changed it into Y'hoshua (יהושע meaning 'Yahweh is salvation') when he sent him to explore the land of Canaan with other eleven men.

Changing a person's name in the Bible is significantly important because it usually happened to establish a new identity. For instance, God changed Abram's name, meaning 'high father' into Abraham, meaning 'father of a multitude' (Genesis 17:5). Importance of changing names can be understood in this way: when people call you by that name, you are reminded of 'who you are' or 'what you should be' if your name has a special meaning, and people continuously engrave your identity on your subconsciousness by calling your name repeatedly.

When the Israelites crossed the Red Sea [Reed Sea], Joshua also walked through the dry ground. He witnessed God drown the Egyptian army and chariots. He also sang the victory song afterwards. He wandered in the wilderness like others and fought for the people of Israel. He went through the same journey just like what the crowd did. So then, what made him different?

As the assistant of Moses, he learnt deep spiritual lessons while waiting on him all the time. He heard what Moses intimately spoke with God (just like conversations between friends) in his tent of meeting outside the camp. He accompanied Moses when he had ascended biblical Mount Sinai to receive the Ten Commandments. As he had descended from the mountain with Moses, he heard people's celebrations around the golden calf. He saw Moses' righteous zeal and wrath for God to destroy the idol by breaking the tablets of the commandments.

After Moses' death, the waters parted at the Jordan River as the people of Israel had for Moses at the Red Sea [Reed Sea]. It was the first wonder that happened under the leadership of Joshua. It was also great surety that Joshua received from God who said to him to be strong and courageous three times in Chapter one of the book of Joshua. Certainly, it was a huge milestone in his spiritual growth as E.E. Cummings says, 'It takes courage to grow up and become who you really are.'

The first battle after the crossing of the Jordan was at Jericho. Joshua led the destruction of Jericho with guidance of God (Jericho March) and then moved on to a small neighboring city Ai. The thrill of victory at Jericho was so quickly replaced with the agony of defeat at Ai. The defeat was a real test of Joshua's leadership through failure. 'How to handle' failure due to either his own or others' faults could powerfully impact on his growth and future leadership. A leader cannot be successful until he or she learns to handle the failure due to either his/her or others' faults.

Joshua, of course, was perplexed by the defeat and catastrophe at Ai. Nonetheless, he immediately tore his clothes and fell to the earth on his face before the ark of the Lord until the evening of the terrible day. Both he and the elders of Israel put dust on their heads for remorse as a sign of Hebrew mourning. At the time of desperation, he cried out to God. Here is his prayer (or are questions) to God for the first time mentioned in the Bible.

> Alas, Sovereign Lord, why did you ever bring this people across the Jordan to deliver us into the hands of the Amorites to destroy us? If only we had been content to stay on the other side of the Jordan! Pardon your servant, Lord. What can I say, now that Israel has been routed by its enemies? The Canaanites and the other people of the country will hear about this and they will surround us and wipe out our name from the earth. What then will you do for your own great name?
>
> - Joshua 7:7-9; NIV -

From Joshua's prayer above we can clearly see that he was fearful to imagine if God won't help him and his people anymore and also concerned about God's reputation damaged by their failure. Yet, his heart was right with God amid such dreadful situation, no matter what. Therefore, God answered, 'Stand up! What are you doing down on your face?' The verb, 'stand up' in Hebrew is *qum* (קוּם), meaning to rise up from a prostrate position for various reasons. In a figurative speech, it is often used for rising as an act of rising out of a state of inaction or failure, for rising to hear Torah, for showing respect and worship, for becoming strong or powerful, for rising up to give deliverance, for assuming an office as a prophet or a judge, and for rising up to give testimony, etc. Thus, God's command here calls for Joshua to rise up from his state of despair and failure in order to prepare himself for action and take up his responsibility by leading the people of Israel in God's deliverance. Surely, he learnt a spiritual lesson:

> Unless the Lord builds the house, the builders labor in vain. Unless the Lord watches over the city, the guards stand watch in vain (Psalm 127:1; NIV).

Again the people of Israel faced an alliance of five Amorite kings (Jerusalem, Hebron, Jarmuth, Lachish, and Eglon). Joshua asked God to cause the sun and moon to stand still at Gibeon, so that he and his army could finish the battle in daylight. According to the record of Jashar, Joshua said to the Lord in the presence of Israel as below:

> 'Sun, stand still over Gibeon,
> and you, moon, over the Valley of Aijalon.'
> So the sun stood still, and the moon stopped,
> till the nation avenged itself on its enemies.

> - Joshua 10:12-13; NIV -

How bravely and courageously Joshua commanded them on that day! It is written, 'There has been no day like it before or since, when *the Lord heeded the voice of a man*, for the Lord fought for Israel' (*Italics mine*, Joshua 10:14; ESV). As a result, the sun and the moon obeyed him. This is the climax of Joshua's spirituality. It obviously shows that he was a man of faith filled with the Holy Spirit and powerfully anointed to declare such commands at that time. He was the man whose voice was heard by God. He was the man who could touch and shake God's heart.

Joshua's influence on the nation of Israel was to continually encourage the people, move and guide them through supernatural impact. Not only his words but also actions brought inspiration to the nation of Israel, spurring them to remain faithful. It can be seen from his final speech when he assembled all the tribes of Israel in order to renew the Mosaic Covenant with them at Shechem.

> Now fear the Lord and serve him with all
> faithfulness. Throw away the gods your ancestors
> worshiped beyond the Euphrates River and in
> Egypt, and serve the Lord. But if serving
> the Lord seems undesirable to you, then choose
> for yourselves this day whom you will serve,
> whether the gods your ancestors served beyond
> the Euphrates, or the gods of the Amorites, in

whose land you are living. But as for me and my household, we will serve the Lord.

- Joshua 24:14-15; NIV -

I began the chapter by describing the benefits of being born and growing up in a Christian home. It was also mentioned that it won't be a blessing until he or she truly encounters God personally. As we are aware of others' life in the Bible (especially Joshua's life), there is a higher chance for him or her to encounter God rather than those who have never been exposed to a Judeo-Christian culture throughout their entire life. What made Joshua special? Well, he obviously did not stay in the status quo of religion or tradition but deepened his intimacy with God as what he had seen and learnt from his predecessor Moses. Also, he learnt spiritual lessons through his own failures. He tasted God's sovereign power through many wars and knew that the battles absolutely belonged to him.

Do you know that God intentionally left the nations in the land of Canaan to teach warfare to the descendants of the Israelites who had not had previous battle experience (Judges 3:1-2)? Supposedly, when we are engaged in war, we should fight to win; otherwise we will lose our life. Needless to say, we become stronger and mightier after war and also experience God's sovereign power in a life-threatening situation. The same applies to spiritual warfare. Our spirit becomes stronger and mightier after war. Our spirit experiences God's sovereign power to win the battle. Our faith becomes rock-solid as we experience the spiritual warfare afterwards.

    I would like to close the chapter to encourage the generation with no experience of war. 'Be bold and be strong. Do not be afraid to engage in spiritual warfare. Remember that the battle belongs to God. Dig your spiritual hunger within and go deeper and draw yourself close to him.'

Three

EVEN IF NOAH, DANIEL, AND JOB

A particular scripture, which I always pondered whenever I read, was Ezekiel 14:14 (NIV), '... even if these three men -Noah, Daniel and Job- were in it, they could save only themselves by their righteousness, declares the sovereign Lord.'

There are many great heroes in the Bible but why God singled out these three men. Why wasn't Abraham included? He willingly gave up his beloved son, Isaac for a burnt offering in obedience when God commanded to sacrifice him for a test. Even was Abraham called God's friend (Isaiah 41:8)? What about Moses? He was the one who received the Ten Commandments directly from God. Even God talked to him like a friend face to face. Why wasn't David mentioned? God called him as 'a man after His own heart?' (1 Samuel 13:14). What about Elijah? He was the one who had a power encounter against the pagan priests of Baal on Mount Carmel. Why not Samuel who interceded for people without ceasing (1 Samuel 12:23)? You name it!

When God chose these three, there must be an obvious reason. Let us first explore the lives of Noah, Daniel, and Job and then their characteristics before getting to the point.

Noah

Noah (נח) is the hero of the biblical flood story as many of us know it. He first appears in Genesis 5:29 as the son of Lamech and the ninth in descent from Adam. He was a righteous man or a man of blameless piety and found favour in the eyes of the Lord (Genesis 6:8). So, when God beheld the corruption of the earth and determined to destroy it, He gave him a divine warning of the impending disaster and made a covenant with him, promising to save him and his family. He was instructed to build an ark for 120 years. In accordance with God's instructions, he took into the ark representatives of every living species from which the stocks might be replenished and multiplied later on.

In particular Apostle Peter mentioned Noah as 'a preacher of righteousness' (2 Peter 2:5). Around Noah's time, the world was 'corrupt in God's sight, and the earth was filled with violence. And God saw the earth, and behold, it was corrupt, for all flesh had corrupted their way on the earth' (Genesis 6:11-12; ESV). Although Peter describes Noah as a preacher, it is more likely translated as either a 'herald' or a 'harbinger.' We can imagine how much Noah suffered amid the corrupt generation with full violence and lawlessness described as below:

> When human beings began to increase in number on the earth and daughters were born to them, the sons of God saw that the daughters of humans were beautiful, and they married any of them they chose. Then the Lord said, 'My Spirit will not contend with humans forever, for they are mortal; their days will be a hundred and twenty years.' The Nephilim were on the earth in those days -and also afterward- when the sons of God went to the daughters of humans and had children by them. They were the heroes of old, men of renown. The Lord saw how great the wickedness of the human race had become on the earth, and that every inclination of the thoughts of the human heart was only evil all the time. The Lord regretted that he had made human beings on the earth, and his heart was deeply troubled. So the Lord said, 'I will wipe from the face of the earth the human race I have created -and with them the animals, the birds and the creatures that move along the ground- for I regret that I have made them' (Genesis 6:1-7; NIV).

Furthermore, Noah was building the ark in the mountain. In people's eyes, what Noah did was an odd and crazy thing because there was no rain or flood before according to the account of Genesis 2:5. What was the driving force behind him to carry on the long-time building project despite ridicule and scorn from his generation? The writer of the book of Hebrew gives us the answer. '*By faith* Noah, when warned about things not yet seen, in holy fear built an ark to save his family. By his faith he condemned the world and became heir of the righteousness that is in keeping with faith' (*Italics mine*, Hebrew 11:7; NIV).

Noah was a man of faith and of blameless piety. He walked faithfully with God (Genesis 6:9) and found a great favour in the eyes of the Lord to inherit the heir of the righteousness for the generation to come.

ε☙

Daniel

Daniel (דניאל) is the hero of and the author of the book of Daniel. His name in Hebrew means 'God is my judge' or 'judge of God.' He was born in Jerusalem and came from a royal or noble family but was transported to Babylon in his youth. When the Babylonians who captured him from Judah wanted to wipe out any identity with his past, they renamed him Belteshazzar, meaning 'may [god] protect his life.' As we read the book of Daniel, we can see the name Daniel throughout the book with the exception of a few occasions (only the pagan king and his mother queen mentioned his Babylonian name Belteshazzar). It shows his strong will to keep his indentify as a Jew, no matter what.

He was a legendary for his wisdom, integrity and faithfulness to God. In Babylon, Daniel and his three Hebrew friends, Shadrach, Meshach, and Abednego were trained in the king's court for service. During the time of their early training, the Babylonians wanted them to eat the king's rich food (meat sacrificed to idols) and wine but they chose vegetables and water instead. At the end of a test period, they were healthier than the others who ate the king's food and wine.

Later on Daniel became an excellent governor, and his court career lasted nearly 70 years because of his extraordinary wisdom and ability to interpret dreams. God made him prosper during the reigns of successive rulers. Yet, he faced the challenge of being thrown into a den of lions due to other advisers' slander and jealousy when king Darius planned to put him in charge of the entire kingdom. Daniel survived in the lions' den because he totally trusted in God. Not only was he alive but he also made the pagan king acknowledge God as a sovereign and a deliverer. It is a great testimony of his faith in the foreign land where the monarch despised the Jews and decimated his own small country of Israel. Nevertheless, Daniel did not hesitate to acknowledge the true God of heaven as his source of wisdom even he was at great risk of death. As a result, king Darius declared that Daniel's God is a far greater king than he, and God's kingdom is much greater than his earthly kingdom.

> I issue a decree that in every part of my kingdom people must fear and reverence the God of Daniel. For he is the living God and he endures forever; his kingdom will not be destroyed, his dominion will never end. He rescues and he saves; he performs signs and wonders in the heavens and on the earth. He has rescued Daniel from the power of the lions.
>
> - Daniel 6:26-27; NIV -

Daniel was a faithful servant of God who set an example to God's people on how to live a holy life. He continuously fixed his eyes on God, no matter what happened.

He was an intercessor to pray ceaselessly for the lost nation in a foreign land. Certainly, Daniel 6:10 (ESV) testifies it: 'When Daniel knew that the document had been signed, he went to his house where he had windows in his upper chamber open toward Jerusalem. He got down on his knees three times a day and prayed and gave thanks before his God, as he had done previously.' As we can see, his prayer pattern was not shaken by such challenge, and his integrity still faithfully remained.

Daniel greatly influenced not only pagan kings but also the Babylonian wise men (enchanters, astrologers, and diviners) or magi down through generations. With great wisdom, he successfully pleaded for the lives of the wise men/magi who had failed to interpret the king's dream (Daniel 2:24). He came to be highly regarded among the magi by saving many of their lives. During the time of King Belshazzar, the fingers of a human hand appeared and wrote on the plaster of the wall at the royal banquet hall. The Babylon wise men summoned by the king failed to read and interpret the writing for the king. Daniel who was grey-headed by then stood before the king and interpreted for him. As a reward, he became the third highest ruler of the Persian Empire (Daniel 5:7).

On a light note, have you ever wondered how the wise men or magi found Jesus in Bethlehem or even knew that he was born to be a king? It is not surprising if we remember that Daniel was both the head of the Babylonian wise men (or the chief Magian) and a top official in the Persian Empire where magi held great political influence.

In history the magi first appear in the seventh century B.C. as a tribe within the Median nation in eastern Mesopotamia. The origins of the magi are also the origins of Abraham (father of a multitude) although the name magi became associated with the hereditary priesthood later on. Their political influence continued to grow until they became the most prominent and powerful advisory class both in the Babylonian and Medo-Persian empires because of their combined knowledge of science, agriculture, mathematics, and history. They were very good at astronomy and astrology.

So, there is no doubt that the magi learnt much from Daniel about the one true God. Apparently, many Jews remained behind in Babylon after the Exile, refusing to go back to Jerusalem. They intermarried with the people of the east which makes it all the more likely that Jewish messianic influence remained strong in that region, even up to New Testament times. After hundreds of years, Daniel's prophecy of the coming Messiah could have been well known to the wise men. Angel Gabriel told Daniel that 'After the sixty-two "sevens," the Anointed One will be put to death and will have nothing. The people of the ruler who will come will destroy the city and the sanctuary. The end will come like a flood: War will continue until the end, and desolations have been decreed' (Daniel 9:26; NIV). This would explain why the magi in the New Testament were able to discern when and where the Messiah was born.

Daniel was a man of faith and integrity. He was a man of blameless piety. He was highly esteemed and greatly loved by God (Daniel 9:23). Also, he was a man of intercession. While praying and fasting, many prophecies including the coming Messiah were revealed to him by angel Gabriel.

ࢋ

Job

Job (איוב) was the wealthiest and most respected of all the men of the east (northern Arabia) and lived with his extended family and vast flocks in the land of Uz. He was blameless and upright, constantly mindful to live in a righteous and godly manner. This is what he did continually. His seven sons often took turns holding feasts in their homes, and they invited their three sisters to eat and drink with them. Whenever the days of feasting were over, Job sent for his children to purify them, rising early in the morning to offer burnt offerings for all of them. In his heart, he thought that perhaps his children had sinned and cursed God unintentionally while feasting (Job 1:4-5).

The story of Job begins with a discourse between God and Satan, mentioning Job to him saying, 'there is no one on earth like him, a man who is blameless and upright, who fears God and shuns evil' (Job 1:8; ESV). For this statement, Satan contended that Job was only righteous because God blessed him generously. Satan dared God that if given the approval to inflict suffering, Job would charge God with wrong and curse Him. God permitted Satan to abuse Job with the exception of sparing his life to test out his brazen claim.

Over the time of one day, four terrible reports were given to Job: his sheep, servants, and ten children all died due to thieving intruders and natural disasters. Job's response to the reports was '[he] arose and tore his robe and shaved his head and fell on the ground and worshiped. And he said, "Naked I came from my mother's womb, and naked shall I return. The Lord gave, and the Lord has taken away; blessed be the name of the Lord"' (Job 1:20-21; ESV).

From Job's confession above, we can tell that he was very religious and deeply spiritual. Furthermore, he was sensitive to the needs of the poor (Job 29:12, 13, 16 and 31:16). He was wise so people sought out for his counsel

(Job 29:21).

Nevertheless, it is worth noting that he was outside the chosen covenant line of Abraham from which the Messiah would come later. Apparently, the oldest book of the Bible, *Book of Job* was found among the Dead Sea Scrolls. According to Bible scholars, Moses wrote it while in Median, implying that this land would give him good background knowledge of the land of Uz. Why then did God choose Moses to write? Through Moses' pen God was careful to record two strands of God's family line: the Mosaic covenant line in the Pentateuch (Moses' five books) and the existence of faithful believers like Job outside the covenant.

Interestingly, Job's thought process is gradually changing throughout the book of Job. In the beginning he understood that he was innocent, yet he suffered terribly. This blew up everything he thought he knew *about God*. Then in his eyes his life seemed to be hopeless even to death (Job 7:8-10). He cried out for a help and longed for a mediator who could intercede for him before God (Job 9:32-33 and 16:18-22). Then he reached to the point of acknowledging God as his redeemer and have an earnest hope of seeing him after death (Job 19:25-26). Even he arrived at the point of an absolute trust in God who knew all about him and also would make his faith pure as gold after affliction (Job 23:10).

While Job was changing in his mind-set, his three friends Eliphaz, Bildad and Zophar didn't shift their attitudes and opinions which caused God to be angry. 'My anger burns against you [Eliphaz] and against your two friends, for you have not spoken of me what is right, as my servant Job has' (Job 42:7). God even would not accept their prayers but requested them to get Job to pray for them instead (Job 42:8).

What made Job different from his three friends? As God said in the beginning of the book of Job, he was outstanding, and no one was like him on the earth. He was righteous and blameless turning away from evil (Job 1:8). Even when his wife brutally told Job, 'Are you still maintaining your integrity? Curse God and die!' he said nothing against God in all this suffering (Job 2:9; NIV). Above all, he feared God (Job 6:14, 13:15-16, 22:4, 23:15, 28:28, 31:35, and 37:24). With a heart of reverence for God, he had never done anything that might offend God. With having reverence for God and shunning evil, he could obey God's sovereignty in trials.

Strangely enough, God neither answered any of Job's questions in relation to his suffering nor explained why he had to go through the affliction but asked him rhetorical questions related to His creation instead. Isn't it odd? On top of it, is there a specific reason that God spoke to Job out of the whirlwind rather than in a still small voice like what He did to Elijah (1 Kings 19:12)? Well, I believe that God did so in order to teach him two things. One is that God is sovereign power and almighty above the horrendous whirlwind. Imagine Job in front of the powerful and dreadful windstorm!

The other is that God himself is beyond all human understanding whose knowledge is limited in understanding of how creation was formed and made by Him. Therefore, we can say that He doesn't need to answer to all our questions, but rather to demand us to absolutely trust and obey Him.

The highlight of the book of Job is Chapter 42:5-6 (ESV), 'I had heard of you by the hearing of the ear, but now my eye sees you; therefore I despise myself, and repent in dust and ashes.' From Job's confession and repentance, through the affliction he truly knew God. Needless to say, his head knowledge about God became his experiential knowledge of God because of his extraordinary encounter with God. Imagine he conversed with God in a rare occasion since a few people like the prophet/seers were able to hear the voice of God or encountered Him in the Old Testament era. In the same vein, what a blessing for a child, who is born and grown up in a Christian home if he or she can confess exactly what Job stated! In this respect, do you agree that affliction comes to us as a blessing in disguise for our spiritual awakening?

As we know, Job's story ends happily. Especially, when he prayed for his friends as instructed, God blessed him and restored his fortunes exactly twice as much as he had before: from 7000 to 14,000 sheep, from 3,000 to 6,000 camels, from 500 to 1,000 yoke of oxen, from 500 to 1,000 female donkeys and another 10 more children (Job 42:10). He lived 140 years and died old and full of years, and even saw his children and their children to the fourth generation.

ই‍্য

When God singled out Noah, Daniel and Job as in Ezekiel 14:14, there must be a common characteristic of these three men. Before getting to the point, let us first look at the previous verses 1-13 of the same chapter.

Some of the idolatrous elders of Israel came to see the prophet Ezekiel. God sternly condemned them, saying, 'Repent and turn away from your idols; turn your faces away from all your abominations' (Ezekiel 14:6; ESV). The land also became corrupt due to their filthy idolatry and did not produce food for people and beasts as a result. And then God continued to say, '... even if these three men -Noah, Daniel, and Job- were in it, their righteousness could deliver only themselves' (Ezekiel 14:14; ESV)

As we have seen so far, the three were men of faith, found a great favour before God, and had gone through hardships (either persecution or affliction), yet they kept their faith truthfully and walked with God continuously. They showed what a righteous life really looks like - *faithfulness to God no matter what*. Moreover, the most outstanding characteristic of the three is their blameless piety and integrity.

The Bible records that Noah was only righteous and blameless in his generation (Genesis 6:9). From Genesis 6:4 we can understand how wicked and morally corrupt world was at the time. The children of the supernatural beings (sons of God) who had married human women became famous heroes and warriors. They were called 'Nephilim' and lived on the earth at that time of Noah. Nonetheless, Noah and his family were different and not mixed with people in such corrupt generation. So, Noah kept himself pure from spiritual adultery. Daniel was determined not to defile himself by eating the food and wine given to him by the king (Daniel 1:8). As mentioned earlier, he (along with his Hebrew friends) did not compromise but kept himself pure from spiritual idolatry. Job was blameless and upright (Job 1:3) because he greatly feared God. Even God himself acknowledged his reverence for him and his unshaken integrity (Job 2:3). Truly his trust in God and fear of him were not shaken whether he had wealth and material possessions or none. Indeed, he came out as pure as gold after God tested him (Job 23:10).

In contrast to people who were ungodly and had no fear for God around the times of the three, all these three men were blameless and morally correct. Does it then make sense that God chose them as perfect examples? They could be the only ones who were qualified for deliverance or salvation as God declared. '… by the fear of the Lord one turns away from evil' (Proverbs 16:6b; ESV). 'The fear of the Lord is the beginning of wisdom' (Proverbs 1:7a; ESV).

Celebration For The Nations

Four

CELEBRATION FOR THE NATIONS

Now is the time to unfold *Celebration For the Nations* (CFTN) which you have been looking forward to. In order to introduce what it is all about, so far I have talked about the importance of the spiritual legacy first. As mentioned earlier, I can say that the DNA of CFTN is truly in the sacrifice of the worshipper to honour God by bringing every knee to bow before Him and every tongue to give praise to Him from different nations and from generation to generation. To my knowledge, one thing has never changed throughout history is that He is longing and looking for ones who truly worship Him. The true worshipper knows how to love Him and His people. 'Anyone who does not love does not know God, because God is love' (1 John 4:8; ESV).

I myself is one who was born and grown up in a Christian home did not know God truly until I encountered him. I did not know the reality of the spiritual realm genuinely until I fiercely engaged in warfare. I did not know power and beauty of worship honestly until I learnt 'how to worship Him.'

Personally, I long to see many arise like Joshua, Noah, Daniel and Job from this generation and the generation to come. Like others written in the book later on, I also began a wonderful journey towards a greater and deeper understanding of worship along with CFTN. While unpacking CFTN hereafter, I hope that the reader also tastes and sees what others experienced in the book, and what God has done through and with CFTN over the course of time.

Have you positioned yourself to receive the blessings ahead? If you are ready, let us get started!

Gail's Story

by Gail Dixon

My name is Gail Dixon, and I have been involved in Mission work through *World Horizons* and *Nations Trust* since 1980. Although I have worked in different nations, the base for both these works is Wales. I have spent much of my life in this beautiful nation.

In 2004, the centenary of the last *Welsh Revival*, the Lord gave me a vision. I saw the most amazing water. The nearest earthly colour would be a deep sapphire. There was light coming from within it. I tried to reach it, but something blocked my hand. I looked up and saw people from many nations all trying to get to the water. I later realised that these were all from nations that had been linked to the 1904 *Welsh Revival*. Then we all heard a voice say,

> 'It's impossible for you to get to the water, but if you sing, the water will break out and come to you!'

Straight away a verse from Scripture came to my mind,

"'Gather the people together and I will give them water' Then Israel sang this song: 'Spring up, O Well! All of you sing to it'" (Numbers 21:16-17).

I received this vision twice on consecutive prayer days with *Nations*. As I talked and prayed with the team and others in the community, we felt that the Lord was asking us to gather people from the nations affected by the *Welsh Revival* of 1904 to worship together in Wales, and unblock the wells of revival that our fathers have dug.

It took three years of prayer, worship and planning to bring together what we called *Celebration for the Nations*. The name came from the man who started the work of both *World Horizons* and *Nations Trust*. It was given to him years earlier in a time of prayer and fasting. He dreamed of nations worshipping together, celebrating what the Lord has done, and celebrating on behalf of those who don't yet have the freedom to do so.

The Lord linked us strongly with South Koreans, who really bought into the vision. The first Celebration was in 2007, which was the centenary of the Korean Revival that started in Pyongyang, now the capital of the most anti-Christian regime in the world, North Korea.

We also drew teams from America, France, Germany, Eritrea, Mizoram and the Khassi Hills, North East India, and China, as well of course as Wales and England. Up to 1,300 people gathered each day in a marquee on the local aptly named 'Festival Fields' to worship the Lord for a week. It was a wonderful time. Hundreds of Koreans came. Some realised that they had never had a personal encounter with the Lord, and found salvation in the tent. One of the St

John's ambulance team gave his heart to the Lord. A homeless man who wandered in received prayer and found salvation, and later had a home and a job.

People were deeply moved by the Lord as we worshipped. There was no preaching (as the Lord had emphasised singing), although Scripture was read and encouragements and prophetic words were released from time to time. Each day there would be people at the edges of the crowd just on their knees in prayer or wonder. Numerous young people date their call to the mission field from that time in the tent. People were healed, though there were no calls for healing. We realised that as we worship, God worked.

I personally had made no plans for after that Celebration in 2007, as I believed that revival would come, and it would be pointless to have planed anything.

However, though lives were changed, and wonderful things happened, there was no great revival that I imagined. To be frank, the sense of God's pleasure with us was unmistakable; nevertheless, we had to cope with the disappointment of our interpretation of God's promise.

Continuation

Over the three years of preparation, a leadership team had built up. As we talked and prayed together we began to understand that we were in a worship intercession for revival. It was not just for something to happen in Wales, but the fulfilment of what the Lord promised in Joel 2:28 (ESV) when He said;

And it shall come to pass afterward,
That I will pour out my spirit on all fresh,
Your sons and your daughters shall prophecy,
your old men shall dream dreams,
and your young men shall see visions.

We realised that we were one small group among thousands, and maybe millions that the Lord was raising up to prepare the way for His coming again. Every prayer of faith, every longing that has reflected His longing throughout the centuries must have their answer.

Thus, we have continued through the years. Regular worship and intercession times happen in both Wales and South Korea. The Lord told us to stay in Wales for seven years first. He then led us to go to South Korea, and Israel and Japan. We were back in Wales again in 2023. Each *Celebration* adds to the intercession. People sacrifice much to join the worship gathering by selling belongings or even giving up jobs. I believe that the Lord sees each offering and receives it on the altar we have built.

He will fulfil His promise. Our part is to worship Him.

This Is My Story

by Hana Ibberson

Have you just asked me how I got involved in CFTN? Alright! Please get aboard and let me take you back to Year 2006.

I arrived at a strange town called Llanelli, one of the preserved counties of Wales in order to conduct a pilot experiment of doctoral research during my first year's study. I was connected with a non-profit organisation, *World Horizons UK* there. Apparently, *World Horizons* has several teams in the UK, France, Spain, Holland, and Germany. *World Horizons UK* is the main centre for recruiting, training, and sending people to work overseas for the kingdom of God.

At that time, there was a group of young people from different nations for training including English language learning. As a research incentive I gave them an intensive 'learner training' in relation to language acquisition. In the mean time, I was also conducting my research experiment on them. During my stay, I divinely got to know a newlywed couple, Qday and Bridget Lee back then. They kindly provided me with accommodation and welcomed me with warm hospitality. In a natural way, I got to know the preliminary plan of launching CFTN and was asked to translate several historical and practical documents into Korean. I was told that the preparation team would expect lots of Koreans from South Korea and even from London for the gathering in the following year. I willingly accepted the request and went back to Colchester, Essex after the research experiment was over. Who could imagine that God orchestrated all things together according to His timeline back then?

Around that time, I was engaged with my husband, Peter and told him about an international worship gathering in summertime. I thought that it would be a great and special experience for both of us since he loves music and would enjoy the atmosphere in the crowd of people from different nations. We gladly agreed to partake in the worship gathering in the following year although we didn't know exactly what it would be at the time.

The first year of CFTN took place on a field nearby the Millennium Coastal Park along with small and big tents and caravans. Live praises and worships were continuously going on in the marquee every morning and evening for a whole week. All of sudden, the small town Llanelli was full with people, and towners with a lovely Welsh accent seemingly enjoyed the hustle and bustle of the foreign crowd in and around town. As for me, it was much joy to awake and start everyday on the field covered in morning dew drops as if my strength was renewed each day like the morning dew (Psalm 110:3). On top of it, the colourful sunsets across the evening sky throughout the week were spectacular as well. Peter and I spent quality time together with relaxing walks on the beach everyday and visiting old sites and pretty villages here and there during the week. We just enjoyed all the things that we could have together from the beautiful countryside with rolling green hills and quaint Welsh villages. Yet, at the time I was unaware that God was preparing me to build my own alter for worship later on.

As recalling all the memory of CFTN over the years, there are many things to talk about. Yet, a few striking and unforgettable occurrences come to my mind.

In the middle of the week of the first CFTN, we were told that there was a cross-shaped cloud in the sky as shown in the picture below. Thankfully Peter didn't miss the precious moment of taking a photo of it.

All of us were highly thrilled about it. It was a quite auspicious sign because of the place where the cloud appeared. It was just above the core centre of witchcraft practice. It seemed to me that God put His mighty sword on the enemy's head, saying that His war was on as we gathered to worship him just like what He did in the story, recorded in 2 Chronicles 20. When the appointed people of Israel began to sing at the head of the army, the Lord set ambushes against the men of Ammon and Moab and Mount Seir, who were invading Judah at the time of King Jehoshaphat, and they were totally wiped out in the fighting.

Needless to say, most of us were really excited about the unusual manifestation in the sky and expected that some extraordinary thing would happen soon or later. Many were saved and healed physically in the meantime; nevertheless the major breakthrough did not happen as expected in 2007.

CFTN continually went on for six more years until the year of 2013 in Wales. In the meantime, many things happened to my family particularly. My husband Peter was fast-growing spiritually and became hungry for more of God. My daughter was growing as a child of CFTN as time passed. We faithfully partook in the gatherings every summer if we could. Ironically, I was worn out physically and gradually became dry and thirsty spiritually in the midst of spiritual feasting. It was just like one who can be thirsty in the midst of a flood.

One of God's characteristics is His mercy. In order to restore my dry spirit, He challenged me to take an hour prayer slot once a month for the nation as part of the national prayer in 2009. To be honest, it was a tough challenge because my daughter was not a sleeping baby at all. She woke me up almost every two hours throughout the night. Every day I was extremely exhausted physically and tried to sleep whenever I was able to do so. Thus, I was very tired and could not set apart a prayer time properly. Nevertheless, I simply said to God, 'I will take an hour slot at 5 am if you let her sleep through while praying.' I boldly took that challenge but was half in doubt by wondering whether she would sleep through for an hour. To my surprise, she was not awake at all whenever I did the prayer slot for six months until December of 2009. Wow! I told God that I would carry on praying not only every month but also every day if He would continuously let her sleep around that time. Guess what? He did so. Can you imagine how much He loves our prayer, no matter what? I learnt that as long as I am determined, He empowers me to do so. It was all about my attitude and determination.

My spirit was recovered from dryness and began to soar like an eagle. As deepening my intimacy with God, one day I heard an inner voice, saying, 'Get started on shofar-blowing.' I first thought that I had heard something wrong. I never tried to blow the shofar before, and Peter could not blow it properly although he was able to make some kind of noises with it. Furthermore, we did not have our own shofar, either.

Around that time in 2011, we regularly went to a (converted) barn in the outskirts of Essex for worship gatherings fortnightly on Sunday evenings. For a purpose of display, there were a menorah (Jewish lamp) and a shofar (horn of an antelope) on the table at the barn. We asked the leaders of the gathering to borrow the shofar. They kindly lent it to us for a while. We got the shofar at least.

On the night of the following day, Peter went to a powerful prayer meeting at a church in London and learnt a lesson: we can demand the enemy to return everything that belonged to us which had been stolen by the enemy. So, on Tuesday morning Peter declared, 'Enemy! Return what you have stolen from us' and then blew the shofar at the end of our family worship and praise. While preparing lunch, Peter got a phone call from his bank, saying that two strange transactions were made without our knowledge which made the bank want to double-check with him. Speechless! It assured me that what I heard was from God.

On Wednesday morning I cried out to God during the time of our family worship and praise, 'Oh, God. Now we clearly know that you want us to blow shofars but the reality is that none of us can really blow them. So, I ask you to send your angels and teach us.' After my cry, Peter began to blow the shofar. Suddenly, the frequency of its sounds was shifted although it was something beyond my ability to describe with human words. Certainly, I was able to discern the anointed shofar sounds. In fact, it took about two full years' training to discern the sound of anointed blowing and release it since then.

For the five consecutive years (2008-2012) we had indoor small-sized *Celebration* in summertime. It was still good to see familiar faces annually, and several families came with their new babies year after year. During the time of *Celebration 2012*, I had an unusual encounter which can be hard to put into words. My family had to go back to Colchester in the middle of the week due to a scheduled viva of mine (a spoken examination for my doctoral degree). I woke up early in the morning and went out for a prayer walk before leaving Wales on that day. There was a lake nearby the hotel where we stayed. I was meditating on Psalm 67 while prayer walking along the lake since the Psalm begins with a prayer of blessing that draws its words from the great priestly blessing in Numbers 6:24-26 which can spread to all the nations and peoples to sing for joy and praise God. Suddenly, the Spirit of the Lord came upon me and strongly demanded me to declare the second verse of *Days of Elijah* song as below:

> *And these are the days of Ezekiel, the dry bones becoming as flesh. And these are the days of your servant David, rebuilding a temple of praise. And there are the days of the harvest, the fields are white in the world. And we are your labourers in your vineyard, declaring the Word of the Lord. Behold He comes riding on the cloud shining like the sun at the trumpet call. Lift your voice, it's the year of jubilee. And out of Zion's hill salvation comes.*

I first hesitated to do so because I knew exactly what it meant. To my knowledge, there had been much discussion among the core preparation team whether they would hold the outdoor gathering in the following year due to its tremendous expense. If we would go for the outdoor gathering, then it meant that we had to go ahead in faith for God's supernatural provision. Therefore, when the Spirit of the Lord anxiously demanded me to do so, it meant something significant in the spiritual realm for a financial breakthrough, didn't it? I was afraid to shout out the lyrics including, '*rebuilding a temple of praise*', was I not? Frankly speaking, my spirit was discontented, even anguished, until the moment that I had to totally surrender to the Spirit and released the declaration from my mouth in faith. At last, I did it in obedience and felt the hot tears running down my face afterwards.

The seventh year of CFTN took place in Wales in 2013. This time it was scheduled for ten days rather than seven days as we had before. The preparation team particularly requested anyone to bring their own shofars for the gathering since it could be the final one. Later on we were told that there were more than 100 shofars in the gathering.

Again, a gigantic marquee was set up on the same field where we gathered for the first time in 2007. This time the marquee was far larger than the one we had before - more than 1,000 people could fit in the space. In the middle of the week, we had a 'Jericho March' around the marquee accompanied by the sounds of Korean traditional instruments (drums, gongs, jings, and jang-goos, etc.), shofars, and banners. All of us went into the marquee after the seventh lap and waited quietly in His presence for a while. Afterwards, we all shouted out the name of Jesus in our own languages at the same time but in unison. It was an absolutely awestruck moment. However, none of us actually knew what was happening outside the marquee at the time. Someone outside saw interesting clouds, forming in shapes of the capital letters of L-O-R-D in the sky and took a picture of it as shown below. Surprisingly, the cloud appeared very near to the spot where the cross-shaped cloud was in 2007.

Thankfully, CFTN continued every summer in South Korea, Japan and Israel for breakthroughs of the nations. Several things changed since then. Some children of CFTN become young adults. More people become the gray-headed and continually carry on the legacy of CFTN far and wide, waiting for the momentum of a great awakening worldwide as God promised through the prophet Joel. It's just like bulbs under the ground are waiting for its full bloom in due season.

As mentioned earlier, I began my journey towards a greater and deeper understanding of worship with CFTN. Even I have spoken on just a few occasions so far, I could definitely say that it has meant so much to me. Why? I have truly learnt to honour God in worship which will last for the rest of my life here on earth and in heaven.

Finally, I would like to wrap up my story here and hopefully will come back with more amazing accounts in the future. For the moment, I am waiting for the great breakthrough and enthusiastic about the next generation, arising to release prophetic words and to have visions and dreams as promised.

Colin and Mavis' Narrative

by Colin and Mavis Harris

The following is a nonfiction account by means of summarising what an amazing couple has witnessed in their faith journey and experienced with CFTN over the years. Here the author as a reporter was privileged to have an interview with them during *Celebration 2023*.

Prayer a Precursor to Pentecost
Acts 1:14

The author was absolutely humbled to see how God orchestrated to bring forth the first Celebration by calling for 'intercession' first, reminiscent of John the Baptist preparing the way of the Lord before the Saviour of the world began His ministry. To my knowledge, several intercession gatherings regardless of size were faithfully carried on here and there over the years prior to *Celebration 2007*. Certainly, this couple, along with others in Wales, has played a significant part in intercession.

Mavis' journey of intercession started in 2002 when women in Cardiff were asked to prepare for a visit by Ann Graham Lotz, Billy Graham's daughter, who was holding a conference in the centre of Cardiff, entitled:

'JUST GIVE ME JESUS.' Mavis was asked to head up 'intercession,' which was a new experience for her. Weekly prayer and worship gatherings of about 20 followed until the event on 20th October, 2003. It was very significant for Cardiff as 5,000 women gathered. There was such a sense of Jesus meeting each one personally at the well in chapter 4 of John's Gospel.

Both of them were so encouraged and knew that they had to continue to pray for the City and for Wales, knowing that the DNA of Wales was to be a 'House of Prayer.' Thus, they were privileged to use the 'upper room' of the offices of E.A. (Evangelical Alliance) Wales, in the centre of Cardiff, and launched *Cardiff Watch* on St. David's Day, 1st March 2004, meeting weekly until the present.

When visiting Cardiff, Gail shared her vision with Mavis. It immediately resonated with her because of Father's invitation in Isaiah 54:2, 'to enlarge the place of your tent.' She never realised the full extent of how powerful it was to pray and worship with other nations.

In 2007, Mavis and Colin attended the Festival Fields for the international 'worship intercession' and carried on continuously every summer in Wales, in South Korea, and in Israel respectively. These are the foundations they believe: 'I AM the God who brought you out of Egypt; worship Me alone' which is the first commandment; number 1 in the top 10 of the Ten Commandments! Also, the 1927 Catechism describes the chief end of Man is to worship God and enjoy Him forever.

Colin and Mavis (above) and the crowd (below)
gathered, celebrating on the beach in 2007

As Colin and Mavis were asked about their experiences with CFTN, here are their statements.

Miracles Happen When We Worship

For Colin, worship is also intercession. It is a means of redigging the 'wells of revival' in Wales. 'God inhabits the praises of His people; He is enthroned, leaning back on the cushions of Praise' (Psalm 22:3; KJV, The Good News and The Message). He pointed out several Bible references related to that. For instance, in the Philippian Jail at midnight, prayer and worship broke the chains (Acts 16:25-34). At Jacob's Well, a Samaritan woman progresses from seeing Jesus as a Jew (John 4:9) and then as a prophet (John 4:19). Finally, when Jesus defines worship, she sees Him as the Messiah (John 4:25).

Colin and Mavis had no doubt that a week of each *Celebration* was 'a sacrifice of praise,' and believed that any such offering to God, He will multiply. Over the years, during CFTN, they have witnessed that hundreds have responded to the altar call to work on the mission field.

While both of them were staying in South Korea for *Celebration 2014*, it was a great privilege to visit the beach where Robert Jermain Thomas, known as the 'First Protestant Martyr in Korea from Wales' landed in 1866 and also to take part in intercession for 'reconciliation and reunification between the North and the South.' In praying for reconciliation, they visited the vacant Railway Station near the demilitarised zone (DMZ) which has prepared an area for 'International Departures' ready for the day when the North and South become one, and trains can depart northward even to every part of Europe.

The following is remarkable records from Colin's personal diary.

> *There was a day that during Celebration 2014, two intercessors went to the Northern beach of Ganghwa Island, where Robert Jermain Thomas, whose wife Caroline had died during a miscarriage two years earlier, was killed and his bibles torn up. They anointed the well, erected there in memory of Robert Jermain Thomas. On the following day, there was hot news about a father and a son making their escape from the North by swimming across 2.8 kilometres of sea to the very beach anointed the day before.*

• • •

> *Another striking news was that some pastors in the South had been asking for the North to allow a mission (praise and prayer) in Pyongyang, the capital of North Korea for three years. Suddenly, they got the permission to go and do the mission. Such is the power of intercession while Celebration was going on around that time in South Korea.*

• • •

> *On Saturday, August 16th 2014, some South Koreans displaced into Eastern Asia by the 1950-53 war, miraculously drove from there to South Korea. It was a triple miracle:*

(1) They drove across China into North Korea, a miracle that they were allowed into North Korea;

(2) It was a miracle that they drove throughout North Korea and were not detained; and

(3) It was a miracle that they drove across the demilitarised zone (DMZ) into South Korea. Normally, nothing is allowed across, not even members of 10 million families split apart by the war.

For Mavis, CFTN has been a great encouragement and blessing as she joined with brothers and sisters from many nations, worshipping together as 'Family.' To her, the word of God seemed to come alive before her eyes, and she became a part of it (Psalm 133). The FREEDOM of the worship was inspirational, as was the PASSION for JESUS amongst the intercessors, particularly when they were out on the fields which certainly shifted the spiritual atmosphere.

Both of them witnessed many were physically healed, and several family lives were changed every summer over the years. They heard of many testimonies from others.

For an outstanding example, a lady who is called by God as an intercessor for many nations was in Israel for *Celebration 2016*. When she was standing on Mount Carmel, she exclaimed that it was the fulfilment of what God said to her before. They said that they have been truly blessed by CFTN over the years because they enhanced their concept of 'worship and intercession' with different denominations and nations.

Mavis (centre) and intercessors at Bible College of Wales

As considering 'how to pass on our spiritual legacy to the next generation,' they were asked about any encouraging or challenging words to talk about.

The Next Generation

Colin is with the Psalmist in Psalm 78 declaring, 'we will tell the next generation about the Lord's power and His great deeds and the wonderful things He has done' (Psalm 78:4; The Good News). So, he taught teenagers in Sunday school for 30 years. That Baptist Sunday School had a 'Decision Sunday' every year. He was keen that teenagers should understand that the Word of God (Bible) is not just one book but a library of 66 books written by over 40 different writers (from kings to fishermen), on 3 different continents, in 2 or 3 different languages over a period of 1,400 years. He assures that the Bible is not about rules, regulations, religion or ritual but 'GOD'S REVELATION LEADING TO RELATIONSHIP.'

For Mavis, she began to say her favourite phrase, 'Caught rather than taught!' And then she continued, 'You can tell your children. You can express it and live it in your family. On a personal level, we have three (now grown-up) children and helped them have a wider exposure to Christianity through different Christian camps like *Spring Harvest*, *Kingdom Faith*, *Stoneleigh*, and *Don Double camps* from a young age.'

During *Celebration*, Mavis could see a hope for the future as multiple generations were worshipping together in one place. It was great for them to see a young worship leader who drove them around while they were in South Korea. Now (in 2023) he is living in Wales and in CFTN with his three young children - the next generation. Some Koreans in Wales, while on Mission, now have young families and are now bringing the next generation up without much support. Especially, Mavis mentioned that a prophetic guy at her local church, who knew nothing about CFTN, saw a picture of 'a bunch of grapes gradually changing into the fullness of its fruit.' He saw this prophetic picture on Sunday just before commencing *Celebration 2023* on the following Monday. She concluded the interview by saying, 'We don't necessarily see the fruit like the great revival(s) in the past but can encourage each other for the big picture of God's plan by simply doing our part. I've been blessed and so encouraged to be part of it through *Celebration*.'

In conclusion, Colin and Mavis' thoughts on CFTN resonated so much with the author since I have thought that what we have done and are doing at present is just like a 'dot-to-dot picture' designed by God. We don't see the whole picture but are connecting one dot to another dot (and even one generation dot to another generation dot) in order to complete the picture which God has already designed. So, it is absolutely right to rejoice with what we have done so far and what we are doing at the moment. Are we not proud of being part of connecting the dots for His picture? In this light, there is no doubt that CFTN has played a great role.

It has been an absolute pleasure to know Colin and Mavis from the beginning of CFTN and have time to find out what God has done through them. As said in the beginning of the book, God is making history through men and women. This precious couple is one who God has used to make His story. The author is so thankful to make their story known to the world.

Joan's Story

by Joan Davies

I had the privilege of being invited to attend *Celebration For The Nations* in Wales by Peter and Hana Ibberson.

I was able to go on five occasions which included the first one (in 2007) in a huge marquee and the final (in 2013) which was in an even larger marquee! I was able to take a friend with me on each occasion. We stayed in a local Bed and Breakfast place and enjoyed fellowship together. On the last occasion some Christians from South Korea were in the same Bed and Breakfast which was a great joy. I still keep in touch with a Korean pastor today through a social networking service!

It was an amazing time! The singing and times of worship were 'out of this world'! The worship was led by different groups from different countries. Many of us waved flags representing different nations during the time of worship. I was amazed that I did not feel tired after waving a flag for a long period of time. At times we stopped singing and prayed together in small groups. My favourite time of prayer was in the early morning before the worship started with some Pentecostal brothers and sisters from Wales. These sessions were arranged in the seventh CFTN.

The march through the town of Llanelli as an outreach activity in the afternoon was also thrilling. Many people were dressed in their colourful national costumes, and tracts and small gifts were given out during that time. Local people stood and stared and were amazed to hear the singing which was accompanied by Korean musical instruments. We gathered in the local park and worshipped God in the open air together.

Worshipping in a local park

On two occasions we were privileged to be in a very large church in Llanelli. Different choirs took part. The high light at this time was listening to two professional Christian opera singers who raised the roof with their voices!

It was a great joy to meet people from many different countries including South Korea, Germany, India, France etc... It was very moving to see several pastors from various countries on the platform together worshipping the Lord.

Celebration at Samuel Centre, Llanelli

There were times of exuberant worship but there was also time of quiet where there was a wonderful sense of the Lord's presence.

It was a joy to know that God was moving in a special way at Victory Church in Cwmbran. It started with when a pastor and an elder were asked to pray for a man in a wheel chair. They prayed and he got up immediately and was healed and many people were astonished. Several others during the next few days were healed and came to know the Lord as their Saviour.[2]

---

[2] Paul Haynes' miraculous healing stunned the congregation in Cwmbran as he leapt from his wheelchair. Visit the website for his story in detail. https://www.newlifepublishing.co.uk/latest-articles/dir-art/wheelchair-healing-marks-outpouring/

We were sad to leave Wales but knew that God in His own time would accomplish His will and purposes for Wales. I visited London shortly after being in Wales and was so pleased to see some of the young people from South Korea handing out tracts in Trafalgar square who we had met in Llanelli!

For me it was a time of great encouragement and fellowship with other Christians from many countries of the world. To God be the glory for what He did and will do through the continuing work of CFTN!

Joan (centre) with her friends, Sara (left) and Jurai (right)

Jessie's Story

by Jessie Ho[3]

My story is a 'spillage' from *Celebration For The Nations*. As some others would have mentioned in their stories, CFTN went on for a wonderful seven years from 2007 to 2013 until Gail decided to draw it to a close, and encouraged the participants to open up 'wells' locally where they reside. *Celebration Colchester* was one of these 'spills' from CFTN.

I moved to Colchester, England from Taiwan for my new job in September 2013. I was a spiritual infant all by myself in a foreign country. I was desperate for spiritual nourishment and longed for spiritual growth. While looking for a home church to settle into, I was invited to serve at an international student ministry on campus (University of Essex) where I met a Taiwanese lady who brought me to the Ibberson family and *Celebration Colchester*. From then on, worshipping God with *Celebration Colchester* every fortnight became my regular nourishment. Honestly, I

---

[3] Jessie's full story and several videos [One Voice performance, the pianist Aija Kim's performance, Father's Love dance, One Voice procession in Druze village, etc.] are available on Nehemiah 9.3 Mission website (Story blog) at https://nehemiah93.com/2016/08/15/celebration-israel/

didn't know much at all about *Celebration Colchester*; one thing I certainly knew was that I love to sing to God. Through *Celebration Colchester*, I learnt the difference between 'singing' and 'worshipping,' and the power that worship carries. I learnt a worship that delights God has no direct correlation with how much I can tangibly feel. I learnt what a shofar is and what it does. I learnt who the Holy Spirit is, and how to hear His voice and partner with Him. I learnt that I just needed to come just as I am with a heart towards God, and eventually God will make me grow.

Indeed, I came and stayed and grew in God's delight and protection for me.

Celebration Israel

Having heard stories after stories around CFTN, I was finally opened to what the 'founding fountain' was like, after a few years. In 2016, I was told that CFTN was having a reunion in Israel. Certainly, I signed up to it in excitement.

After months of waiting, I finally got on my flight from New Zealand to Israel, and eventually arrived at Mount Carmel in Haifa. The venue for *Celebration Israel* that year was set at the Mount Carmel Conference Centre (Kehilat HaCarmel) in a village called *Druze*.

Everyday there were worship and intercessions in the afternoon and evening except the 12-hour worship on

Wednesday from 10 am to 10 pm. The worship teams from various countries such as Israel, Wales, England, South Korea, Japan, China and France took turns to lead the worship in 1.5 hour slots each day.

It was certainly a rare opportunity to take off a whole week from work and just do nothing much but worshipping God. So, it was also certainly a highly sensational and ultra enjoyable experience.

Jessie (centre) with the Ibberson Family (left) and the Lee family (right) and Gail (front) at Kehilat HaCarmel

There were different styles of worship. For instance, different languages were spoken, different musical instruments were played, various genres of songs were sung and different forms of worship were there although there was one common denominator, i.e. honouring God. Here I saw various forms of worship and praise such as singing songs with full lyrics, singing songs with minimal words and even without words, dancing, and playing instruments.

Of note, there was a Korean worship team, 'One Voice', who had developed Korean traditional dance and music into a worship form for the Lord. I heard the members of this particular group were entirely living by faith, who brought their talents together solely for the purpose of worshipping God. I was really touched by their devotion and faith to God, and really prayed in my heart that I could have such a pure heart of worship for the days of my life too.

The week seemed short and had gone quickly. I remember a Messianic Jewish attendee said, 'For the first time, the Gentiles made me jealous!' I simply prayed to God, 'Let this not be a once-a-year or one-off experience; let our heart of worship not be left behind in Israel; allow us to cherish the joy and honour of worshipping God with our first love and to live our life in such a way all the time.'

My Song of Songs

by Sora Kim

Shalom! My name is Sora Kim. I used to be a singer of (Korean) *Flow* worship team.

It was the year of 2010 which I had to go back to my hometown from a different part of South Korea due to my family issues. One day the worship team leader of *Flow*, Pastor Lee suggested me to join *Celebration 2012* in Wales. Although it sounded very inviting, I didn't consider the UK as a nation for Mission. Moreover, there was an opportunity to join another mission for Myanmar. Hence, I kindly declined his invite. Then he said, 'Remember London Olympics in 2012!' Immediately, my mind flashed back to the day in 2008 about four years ago.

While I was watching the closing ceremony of Beijing Olympics on TV, I had an odd experience at that time. I noticed a lady on the rooftop of a red bus from a virtual foretaste video of London Olympics. While she was waving her hand, a big ball was rolling around. As I saw this, I started sobbing without knowing a reason. From time to time, when God wanted to do something for my life in the past, He impressed me with such phenomenon - crying with no reason. So, I humbly knelt down and asked, 'God, why am I crying? I don't understand why I am crying now.

I don't particularly like the UK, nor do I love sports,' but simply prayed, 'is there a specific reason to go to the UK? If so, send me, Lord!

Since then I got involved in several missions and studied abroad, nevertheless, I totally forgot about that incident until the moment which Pastor Lee shouted at me, 'London Olympics 2012 is this year!' Again, I began to think to myself, saying, 'Surely, I will go to the UK.' However, I couldn't tell him that I would join the team for *Celebration*. On one hand, I continued to pray that God's will be done in my life over this matter.

Strangely enough, all things went smoothly in terms of my preparation for *Celebration* as if God was quickly getting rid of all the obstacles and seemingly pushing me to a getaway. Surprisingly, I was able to get a ticket just before a week of my departure. Surely, there was no doubt of His intervention at the moment.

My Celebrations For the Nations

My first *Celebration* was the year of 2012 at Samuel Centre in Wales. I partook in it as a singer of the worship team although I had to go back to Korea in the middle of the week. I never forget the precious moment of worship with the brothers and sisters from North Korea. I was so thrilled and saw the true meaning of worship among them since they were the ones who once had risked their life to escape from the North. Certainly, I sensed in my spirit that I would return to Wales for the following year.

My second *Celebration* happened outside in the field in 2013. Especially, several things occurred to me in that year. First, I had to quit my job to come to Wales. Also, I had extraordinary experiences while touring London, France and Italy after *Celebration* was over. To my surprise, God had already prepared a new job for me when I went back to Korea afterwards. I got connected coincidently with a team member of *Wild Step* who worked for a Christian school in Korea at the time. I didn't know about it before but simply applied for the job post as I had found it from a want ad in the paper. While talking over the phone, I figured out that person was the same one whom I got to know during *Celebration*.

Going back to *Celebration 2013*, the big marquee was set up on the beautiful field ground. Personally, it was very challenging for me to stay in the tent with others because I couldn't sleep properly due to the extreme coldness at night and had cold showers as the hot water ran out. When the sun rose in the morning, I was just able to sleep while worship music was playing on. Nevertheless, it was the greatest time of my life. If I were asked whether I would do it again in the future, to be totally honest, I would say 'No' to that.

Anyway, my brother-in-law prayed for me before leaving Korea and said, 'God spoke to me that you will have pain on your knees but you shouldn't worry about it because He will heal you. And try to memorise the book of Song of Songs as your Rhema words.' So, I read the Song of Songs every day.

As expected, one day there was pain on my knees in the midst of worship and praise. Even I couldn't kneel down properly due to excruciating pain. The only way I could worship God was that I first fold my left limb at the entrance of the marquee and then put my right leg next to it together with a help of my hands. In the meantime of struggling with pain, I was told that there was a couple, Peter and Hana Ibberson who were interceding for people. Promptly, I met them, and they prayed for my knees. The pain was gone afterwards.

After *Celebration* was over, all of *Flow* team members were staying in London for a while. I shared a room with three other girls. We had time of cooperative prayer at night. One of us started to confess her sins, and we continued to pray and fought against the evil spirits when they had manifested. After the evil spirits had left from us, we began to see visions and received the prophetic words from the Lord. I thought that we just prayed for a couple of hours but it was already morning.

We visited *The Chapel, Museum and John Wesley's House* on that day. At that time I had no knowledge of the Methodist, but I only remember what Pastor Lee said, 'We should inherit the nature of Wesley' love and compassion.'

Recalling of *Celebration 2013*, there was a strong message for North Korea in that year. Personally, I got a calling for the nation of Israel. I also applied for the outreach for Spain organised by *Wild Step* after *Celebration,* but it was called off. Thus, I alone did a spiritual mapping in France and Italy; especially, I longed for visiting the Catacomb.

While staying in France, I began to spot several Jews and wept whenever I saw them. On the following day, I was looking and praying for accommodation for a longer stay. An address in my diary caught my eyes. Some time ago, someone gave me the address but I totally forgot about it. The place was situated in a suburb. I sort of felt that God was guiding me to that place, eventually I got there. It was a kind of guest house to pay for staying there. However, the house host told me that I could stay without paying as God instructed him. The host was the first Korean missionary to France. He kindly enough took me to several historic sites and told me about important histories related to the sites. God opened my spiritual eyes to see the captivity and restoration of the cathedral and ongoing spiritual warfare there. Indeed, I understood the spiritual aspects of France and got the divine connection.

With a great expectation, I arrived in Rome to visit the Catacomb. When I got on the metro, tears came down on my face without a reason. I just pondered that I was weeping because of the blood of the martyrdom in the past.

The following is a remarkable story of encountering a Jew called Matthew. I met him in Firenze. He was an American-born Jewish but never visited Israel. As I arrived at the accommodation in Firenze, I understood that all the rooms were fully booked. So, I had to move to a three-bed room which looked better than the one I had temporarily booked before. There was no one in that room when I went in. I slept very well on that night. On the following Sunday morning I was preparing myself for a church service. Suddenly, I was so prompt in praying and continued to pray for two hours. In the meantime, I sensed that God was preparing me for something important.

I arrived at the church building an hour early because I mistakenly saw the time. I felt that I was quite familiar with the church yard of the grape vines and pomegranates because it resonated with the book of Song of Songs -

especially, chapter 7 which was my day's devotion on that day while reading. What a surprise!

While listening to the sermon, 1 Peter 3:15 (KJV) was ringing in my mind as Rehma words. 'But sanctify the Lord God in your hearts: and be ready always to give an answer to every man that asketh you a reason of the hope that is in you with meekness and fear.' Immediately, I took a note of it and then thought to myself seriously that I should prepare to share the Gospel message with the attitude of meekness and fear.

When I came back to the accommodation after service, I noticed several comics of *Dragon Ball* on the top bed at the left corner of the bedroom. Immediately, I began to worry about the situation where I was in, thinking 'I have to share the room with a strange man.' However, I decided to sleep quickly and then closed my eyes. At that moment, the door of the room was widely opened. Then I quickly opened my eyes and raised my right hand, saying 'Hi' with a big smile. I didn't understand why I responded to him in that way at that time, but I felt that I should talk to him. The only topic which I could think of was the thing that I had done for the day. So, I opened my mouth to say, 'I have been in a church today because it is Sunday. What about you? Have you been in the church today?' For my question, he gave me a cold shoulder, saying, 'I'm Jewish.'

Strangely enough, I continued to talk to him with words of blessings not likely what I used to do before, that is, speaking in tongues against the enemy as if I was engaged in spiritual warfare. At the time, my eyes were full of tears, and my lips were full of blessings! Also, I said, 'Don't you know that you (plural) are the blessed people? God loves your people so much.' He was very surprised by my words, saying, 'I have never heard of such words from a Christian before.' I felt ashamed and apologised to him and his people on behalf of Christians and kept weeping. I myself couldn't understand why I was weeping and even talking like that. He told me that he didn't know Jesus. So, I began to share the Gospel message with him. I explained to him with a simple metaphor of an ant. 'Imagine you are watching an ant that is coming closer to a puddle. The ant cannot understand your warning for the coming disaster even if you would shout at it. The only way you can save the ant is becoming an ant. It is the same with Jesus. To save us from the eternal destruction, Jesus who is God came to the world as a human being so that you and I can understand Him.' Then he was puzzled and asked me why I was telling him like that. I replied that it just came to my mind at the time. He was quite surprised at my words and told me that it was his life-long thought but he had never talked about it with others.

Interestingly, Matthew's itinerary started from Milan, the North of Italy to Venice via Firenze to Rome whereas mine began in reverse order from Rome to Firenze via Venice to Milan. The accommodation in Venice that he booked was the same that I had booked for mine which I was meant to go on the following day. He felt strange as he compared the printed version of his itinerary with mine.

I was about to sleep after sharing the words of Isaiah. Matthew said that he got a crick in his neck. I offered him a prayer for healing and prayed in Jesus' name. On the following day, I gave him a piece of paper with several prophetic words (about Jesus) in the Old Testament and a souvenir. Somehow I called off the rest of my itinerary and went back to Korea.

Since then God prepared me for the nation of Israel for two years. (Later on I was sent to Israel for a missionary work as God told me about my ministry there.) In the meantime, I continuously prayed for Israel in tears and had a chance to visit there for just one day during the Full Moon Fest (*Chooksuk* in Korean) as I worked for a company at the time. I got connected with people at a newly planted church (only 6 days old at that time) in Israel and stayed there on Shabbat day. Afterwards, as soon as I arrived at the airport in Korea, I got a notification (on my mobile phone) from the *Flow* chat room. Interestingly, there was an announcement sent by a church in Seoul under the name of the united ministry among global churches. The name of the church in Israel where I stayed was on the list of the churches. Later on I was told that the church was just planted according to God's plan. Soon after, I was sent by a local church in Korea to join their ministry as a collaborative missionary for two years. In the meantime, I was continuously trained and guided by God. The following are my significant memoir during the time in Israel:

On Mount Carmel in 2016

There was a serious warfare. Several worship teams couldn't make it if there were no breakthroughs. I sensed heavy darkness, covered over our worship place. It has never been like that before since I have partaken in Celebration. There should be a great breakthrough.

On Mount Carmel in 2017

I have been continuously engaged in fierce warfare. I could see the reality during Celebration. There were several team members who had lost their beloved ones and buried them before leaving Korea. Even Gail said that her honourable leader just passed away and was in bereavement.

Today what Pastor Joseph said on the stage resonated with me so much, 'Brothers and sisters. Please remember this: your today's worship could be the tomorrow's worship for someone else who longed for but is no longer here.'

On the following day, there was an incident of suicide. We were told that a North Korean defector threw himself into the sea of Galilee. The massive healing for trauma has just begun.

On the following morning, a lady defector from the North saw me and asked me, 'Are you serving in a worship team today?' 'Yes, I am' I replied. Then she said that she got terrible news of her mother's death in the North in the morning. Immediately, my heart was broken. I tightly embraced her and wept together.

In the meantime, there was an ongoing investigation and searching for the dead body of the defector. There were serious discussions on 'whether we should carry on Celebration or stop now.' I have been struggling, too. A thought of 'How can I worship with emotional pain?' has

> continuously bothered me. Then I noticed a smiley face of the lady who had told me about her mother's death in the morning. To my surprise, she was jumping and rejoicing before God in front of my eyes. Wow! It really hit me. 'Is there any other reason not to worship God? Look at her! Even she does it with all her might!' So, I did my best for God today.

While I was in Israel, God told me that He set me (as His servant) apart for a mission so I should take a course at a Methodist seminary. As I mentioned earlier, I had no knowledge of the Methodist at the time. So, I asked Him for confirmation. At night, God reminded me of the visit to *The Chapel, Museum and John Wesley's House* in 2013 while I was praying. On the following early morning, He again reminded me of *Celebration 2015* in Korea. I didn't know where the venue was at the time. Later on I found out that it was the Methodist Seminary. Surely, God was pointing me to the same direction with these two inspirations, that is, *the Methodist*. Finally, God confirmed me with a dream. So, I rushed to go back to Korea and took M.Div. (Master of Divinity) course.

During *Celebration 2018* in Korea, I got an inspiration that Japan would host CFTN in the following year. Somehow one day I noticed a wrapped flag next to my seat. When I opened it, it was Japanese flag. I prophetically said to the rest of our worship team members, 'Guys, we will go to Japan for the next *Celebration*.'

In the meantime, Gail was staying in Gwangju (South Korea's sixth-largest metropolis), I translated for her. One day in our conversation, she said, 'we might do next

Celebration in a spiritually very dark place.' Immediately, I thought of 'Japan' again. Of course, the next *Celebration* was planned for Japan. It meant that I should go there.

My heart for *Celebration 2019* in Japan was quite different from the ones in the past. The reason was that I had bad experiences when I had gone to Japan for the business purpose in the past. At the time I struggled with storms and floods and even got stuck in a mountain. Moreover, I had continuous headaches when I saw several shrines and idols in the streets. To be honest, I usually considered myself not sensitive to the dark world, but I had spiritually a negative impression with those abominations. Strangely enough, since then I had dreamed of dreams of going back to Japan several times which made me think of going to Japan again.

Arriving in Japan for *Celebration 2019*, it looked a totally different land this time. Whenever I saw Japanese people, my eyes were full of tears. They looked so lovely and kind. They were so precious souls of God. To me, it was such revelation: my attitude towards the Japanese was contrary to the one that I had before as I obediently responded to God's invitation.

When it came to *Celebration 2023*, my heart was not in it. The reason was that I had already guided a youth group in the land of Israel about a year ago and had many challenges at the time. Furthermore, the dates seemed to clash with my teachers' training and retreat. Nevertheless, I prayed that if partaking *Celebration* was God's plan, then His will be done. And then I left it to Him.

One night, I had a dream. A teacher colleague of mine was piloting a boat. I was in that boat, too. A huge wave hit the boat and lifted it up high in the air. The wave began to wind around the stern of the boat, hence, it was about to sink down from the air. At the moment, there were many people, swimming in the sea. When they saw the boat, they shouted at each other to escape unhurt. Strangely, they were not terrified but looked cheerful. At last, the boat landed safely on the surface of the sea. My colleague then said, 'Look! There is a well under the woman,' as she pointed at the floating glassy building on my right side. Three women who looked like mannequins were there. Indeed, there was the well with a cover underneath one of them who was short in stature at the left. Then a scene changed.

I saw a female teacher in that building who tried to draw the water from the well. I told her that I could draw the water because we needed it. I first sipped some and then gave my colleague the rest to drink. (Later on I was sharing this dream with my close friend. In the meantime, I noticed three female teachers in a staff's room at school. They were sitting on a three-seater sofa. The one who was sitting on the left end was shorter in stature than the others.) When I woke up from this dream, one thing that came across my mind immediately was 'O Well Spring up!' So, I spoke to myself, 'Perhaps I will go for *Celebration 2023.*' Doubtlessly, God made all things possible in preparation for *Celebration* through the school leadership. Especially, interesting things happened in relation to buying tickets.

One day I was watching a movie. In the beginning of the film, it said, '**We need to detour to Cardiff Airport due to the closure of Dublin Airport**.' To be honest, I didn't know the fact that there is an airport in Wales. So, I began to look for tickets to Cardiff Airport. To my surprise, at the end of the film, it said, '**It is a good sign to get engaged on Sunday. We'll dig a well after travelling**.' Wow! It was confirmation for my trip for *Celebration*. Actually, as soon as I was told about *Celebration 2023* in Wales, I was strongly assured that it was meant for 'bringing up the next generation.' Truly, God allowed me to see it with my own eyes. Even it still continues after *Celebration 2023* as I currently work at school.

Finally, I would like to close my story with this: I have realised that many parts of my life journey cannot be explained without *Celebration* since I partook in it. Whenever I was with *Celebration*, God strongly led me each time. It has greatly impacted my past life and also does on the present life and will do on the future life. I don't doubt about it because I truly have tasted it. Especially, I know that He has called me as a missionary for the nation of Israel and assigned me to connect with other nations. I know that He still makes a way for me.

Our Talk On CFTN 2023

by Peter and Hana Ibberson

Hana Here we came back from Wales. We have been refreshed so much, haven't we?

Peter Certainly! After some years' gap it was great to resume *Celebration* this year.

Hana It was! I was emotional to go back to Wales this time since it is definitely your spiritual birthplace, isn't it? You can tell the reader more about it.

Peter I have a Christian upbringing, attending a church that does not believe in the gifts of the Spirit for today. However, I do really love Christian music. When I got to know about CFTN from you, I was happy to go along for the first year in 2007. At this point in time we were engaged. You had tried praying with me at Pentecost Sunday prior to *Celebration* to receive the power of the Holy Spirit, but I couldn't make it although you didn't give up on me. And then we agreed to go to Wales. So I really enjoyed the times of worship that we had throughout the week. You were with me constantly from the beginning of Friday evening through to the following week of Friday morning except Thursday evening when you were already asked (by the preparation team) to do translation on stage. On that Thursday morning I had already said out loud to you, 'I'm ready to receive the Holy Spirit.' So in the evening while you were on stage, I had a powerful encounter with God. It caused me to first of all break down in repentance. After that, Gareth who is part of the Welsh worship team started to sing a spontaneous song related to the verse of Numbers 21, 'Spring up, O well.' I picked up the song very quickly. As I sung it, my tongue loosed and started to sing in tongues. I later spoke with you, and then you replied back to me, 'God told me to pray for him at that moment.'

In the third year my spirit had totally dried up as both of us were still attending the same church. On Tuesday morning I approached an Eritrean pastor who was part of the ministry team to ask him to pray for me. He agreed, and then we went into a side room. When he prayed, his prayer was powerful as God touched me in the centre of my chest. I felt like liquid fire spreading throughout my whole body. With that touch I was so alive and filled with God's presence continually and didn't even need to sleep, and my days at work were still so energetic after CFTN was over. My life had changed so much since then. I would be praying in tongues throughout the whole night. Also, from that experience I would then be asking God to speak to me literally anytime, and then by Saturday night at home my prayer had been answered as I heard God literally speak to me in an audible voice from Ephesians 6 regarding the armour of God. From that I concluded, 'I will live a Holy life and keep on praying and reading my Bible.'

Hana   You do remember the scent that we did smell inside the big marquee in 2013, don't you?

Peter   It happened that the 12-hour worship was ceaselessly going on in the marquee. We were in and out from there; whenever we had to bless people, we were outside the marquee. Approaching to the end of the 12-hour worship, I entered into the marquee first. I smelt a scent like cinnamon. Then I grabbed your hand and asked you come and see. You said you could also smell it because it was very strong scent. Then we asked others whether they could smell it. Strangely, they couldn't. Since then we were able to smell the cinnamon scent from time to time as we were in a spirit-filled worship atmosphere.

Hana   Yea. I miss that so much. Well… there are always amazing things to talk about every time whenever *Celebration* was on. Perhaps we can talk about a few fascinating things of *Celebration 2023*, can't we?

Peter   Let's begin with the lady whom we blessed.

K.R. was struggling with her worship team members in term of interpersonal relationship. Other ladies were jealous of her and even badmouthed her. She was very stressed and restless until the moment we ministered to her. You had to break the curse over her, and then I blew my shofar for her.

Hana   Yea. You usually use the shofar which produces 'G' sound whenever we bless others. But I noticed that you were holding the 'jumbo' shofar at that time. Strangely, I thought that you could blow a high-pitch sound but didn't mention it and left it to the Holy Spirit.

Peter   Actually yes, prior to our ministering to K.R. I had been using the jumbo shofar which I do not usually use as it is a little more difficult for me to blow but was matching the key that the worship was in. So, for me when blowing over her I felt led by the Holy Spirit to have a long sound then go high but the sound did not come out as I intended. It was like an accidental hiccup sound with the shofar. I then looked at her in the embarrassing moment and noticed she gave a startled look. According to her words afterwards, she said the long sound felt like sucking out from her and the high pitch (hiccup) sound was like a gunshot. We were told from her friend later on that K.R.'s relationship was totally restored after that ministry.

         Another one is the couple who was almost

falling apart in their relationship due to the continued arguments. At the end of the evening session, one of the meeting hosts asked us to blow our shofars in the frontline. We and another lady blew the shofars as if we were engaged in spiritual war. We were told that some kind of spirit left from the husband at the sounds of the shofar.

Hana   Yes. I happened to encounter the wife on the following day although I didn't know that she was the other half of the man from that night. She looked so downhearted, and her countenance was dark. Strangely enough I approached her and asked her whether I could give her a big hug since I saw her broken heart with my spiritual eyes. She nodded even though I was a total stranger to her at that time. As soon as I embraced her with my open arms, the word of knowledge came to me. When I said to her all the words given to me, she started sobbing. She said, 'I came here (despite paying such expensive air ticket) to hear this.' She was melted in God's comfort and love. Her countenance was absolutely changed since then.

Hana   Do you remember the lady whom we call her *Mary Llanelli*?

Peter   Yes. What about her?

Hana   I have got a very important spiritual insight from God. I first noticed her when she had screamed during one of the evening sessions. A few folks immediately calmed her down and prayed over her. She seemed to be Okay afterwards. Then I saw her again on the following morning. Actually, I didn't know that she was behind me while I was thoroughly engaging in praise and worship although I was aware of which she was singing with us at the back. Interestingly, she sang from the top of her lungs in broken English. Even I saw some young guys chuckled because of her singing. Of course I knew that she was singing by heart because she couldn't read the lyrics on screen. On top of it, most of the worship songs were new to her. Consequently, her loud singing was obviously not in tune. A few minutes later when my spirit sensed a kind of evil spirit behind me, I immediately turned around to look at who was there. *Mary Llanelli* was behind me! She was quiet at the moment. When I saw her, I felt sorry for her because she was bounded with the evil spirit. As we carried on praise and worship, I heard her loud singing behind. At the very moment I began to smell the cinnamon scent like what we did in the marquee in 2013. It blew my mind for a moment. It was clear that the sound of her singing was pleasing and sweet in God's ears because she did it with her whole heart. Who could deny it? Seemingly, it was the true worship with which God was pleased because He did not reject her broken and repentant heart as Psalm 51:17 says.

Peter   You'd better to tell the reader why we called her *Mary Llanelli*.

Hana   Right! On our way back home I was thinking of her again and wondered what kind of life she has lived. Debbie (our daughter) said to me that she saw a long scar on her right arm. Seemingly, her life in the streets was very tough. She had to fight and defend herself as much as she could as if her husky voice approved. So, her life reminds us of Mary Magdalene's from the Bible - a tough, promiscuous and demonic influenced life! Does it mean that *Mary Llanelli* could be Mary Magdalene if she would meet Jesus? Would it be better to pray for her future then? Hope that we can meet her again. By the way, I think we have talked enough and better to stop here. Do you have anything else to say?

Peter   I hope that the reader can also experience amazing things more than what we have tasted and seen so far.

Five

YOUR BODY SYMPHONY FOR GOD

A symphony is a long piece of music for an orchestra, composed of four movements. Today, I have chosen Ludwig von Beethoven's Symphony No. 9 to play at the moment of writing. The Symphony No. 9 as known *The Choral Symphony* is widely considered the crowning achievement of Beethoven's life. It stretched the boundaries of musical form and structure of symphony. Although it follows the traditional four-movement configuration, it is far longer than any symphony, that is, lasting over an hour in performance. Especially, the final movement of the symphony features four vocal soloists and a chorus, *Ode to Joy* which words were first taken from Friedrich Schilker's poem in 1785 and revised by Beethoven in 1803.

The Symphony No. 9 is still one of the most frequently played orchestral pieces in the world. There is something special about it as opposed to other pieces of symphonies written by Beethoven himself and other composers - a very unique piece of music which no other work can deliver the same powerful message as the ninth does. For instance, it was performed to celebrate the fall of the Berlin Wall in 1989. In addition, *Ode to Joy* has become the EU Anthem since 1985 because of its celebratory poem addressing the unity of all mankind. The ninth is the final brilliant masterpiece of Beethoven as numerous reviewers and commentators agree saying, 'the culmination of its author's genius' or 'the symphony to end all symphonies.' Ironically, he himself could neither hear the applause of the audience nor see their ovations when he performed it.

While listening to the Symphony No. 9, I am fairly thrilled and surrounded by such magnificent and majestic sounds which seem to resonate very much with Beethoven's heart and life. For the ninth, the following instruments are scored for an orchestra: woodwinds (piccolo, flutes, oboes, clarinets, bassoons, and contrabassoon), brass (horns, trumpets, and trombones), percussion (timpani, bass drum, triangle, and cymbals), strings (violins, violas, cellos, and double basses), and *voices* (soprano solo, alto solo, tenor solo, baritone solo, and choir). Its unique feature is the fourth movement accompanied by vocal sounds and more instruments which are not played in the previous three movements. I reckon that Beethoven expressed his whole being by means of producing all sounds on earth in harmony as many as he could put in for glorifying God. Imagine the sounds in his head that were finally released after his life-long toil and sweat, although he couldn't hear it in his life time. He was truly born for music and lived with music and then died; nonetheless, his works still remain after he had gone.

Recently, God has inspired me that we can also produce and perform a symphony with our body in His presence. It was a strange concept to grasp at first. The following is how I finally got to understand 'performing a symphony with the body' as God gradually revealed to me.

Ezekiel 28:12-19 and Isaiah 14:12-15 are generally accepted as key passages, describing Satan before he fell. Satan was the 'anointed cherub' (Ezekiel 28:14). He was beautifully adorned with every precious jewel (Ezekiel 28:13). Nevertheless, the scriptures do not say clearly about his duty in heaven although many believe that he could be the head musician or the chief worship leader. Considering the fact that the angels constantly worship God (Isaiah 6:3; Revelation 4:8), perhaps we can assume that he led that worship. Interestingly, according to Ezekiel 28:13 (NASB), the musical instruments (i.e., drum and pipe) were built in him when he was created, '…the workmanship of thy tabrets and of thy pipes was in thee; in the day that thou wast created they were prepared.' The tabret is a small drum like a tabor especially used in the Middle Ages, struck with one hand whereas the other held a three-holed pipe. Imagine the sounds that Satan made whenever and wherever he moved around because of the built-in instruments in him. According to the scriptures, he was a perfect beauty outwardly and also music sounds overflowed from within him. Then perhaps we can think of a possibility that God has also put the same kind of instruments (not just only singing as an instrument) in us like what he did to Satan.

Not too long ago, scientific research has shown an interesting fact to support my assumption. 'Different cells within our bodies vibrate at different frequencies to create our own "special song." In the presence of acute or chronic illnesses, these vibrations change. They are also altered by things that we eat and do. The higher the frequency, the lighter and healthier the person.'[4]

In this light, it makes sense to us that sound therapy as a means for self-healing within the body has been used to treat some ailments like insomnia, anxiety, depression, and nerve system disorders. It is generally believed that optimal frequency in our body is in order when we are in balance. Our body vibration is in unison with the law of vibration when we are in tune because each cell of our body vibrates at the frequency as it is designed to be. Our thoughts are vibrations so we can change our perception by changing our frequency.[5]

A popular American theoretical physicist and a professor of the City College of New York and CUNY Graduate Center and co-founder of *String Field Theory*, Dr. Michio Kaku also claims this:

> 'In string theory, all particles are vibrations on a tiny rubber band; physics is the harmonies on the string; chemistry is the melodies we play on vibrating strings; the universe is a symphony of strings, and the "Mind of God" is cosmic music

---

[4] Cited from *The Vibrational Frequencies of the Human Body* at https://www.researchgate.net/publication/354326235_The_Vibrational_Frequencies_of_the_Human_Body
[5] ibid.

resonating in 11 dimensional hyperspace.'

And he continues to say,

'What is the universe? The universe is a symphony of vibrating strings. We are nothing but melodies...we are nothing, but cosmic music played on vibrating strings and membranes.'[6]

It is a fascinating discovery, isn't it? It sounds to me that our body frequencies are meant to harmonize with the symphony of the universe. In this regard, if our body is continuously releasing frequencies even without acknowledging them, why don't we deliberately let it out as a symphony (sounds in harmony) for a specific purpose? As far as we are concerned, we are mainly created for glorying God. Remember what Apostle Paul says, '… to present your bodies as a living and holy sacrifice, acceptable to God, which is your spiritual service of worship' (Romans 12:1; NASB). Why don't we consider presenting our body before God as a symphony? This is an example of how I enjoy personally the presence of God.

Step 1

I imagine that I stand before God as an orchestra conductor and position myself in a wide space or room. Where I position myself is so much related to my expectancy. For instance, Moses positioned himself in the place (in the cleft) nearby God as He

---

[6] https://mkaku.org/home/tag/string-theory/

instructed him (Exodus 33:21). Why did God point to the cleft where Moses could be? It was the place where he was very near to Him and could see His back in glory. Remember God instructed him where he should have been positioned! I often imagine that I will perform my own special symphony for God before Him and even other audiences in heaven.

Step 2

I invite the Holy Spirit to come and minister to me. Then I command my body portals[7] to open up and to be ready in order to release sounds (frequencies) of the symphony.

Step 3

In a quiet mood and stillness, I command all body cells from the top of my head to the tip of my toes to release each sound in harmony. My body movements are not the same each time but usually begin with a slow movement and then increase the speed to a bit fast movement and then much faster movements mixed with slow movements in between and the fastest movement in the end.

Step 4

The finale always ends with reciting the Lord's

---

[7] According to *Power Portals* by Joshua Mills, we can connect to the spirit realm by opening up our body portals like eyes, ears, mouth, heart, hands, and feet.

Pray (the prayer that Jesus taught His disciples) in Hebrew and blowing our kudu horn (long) shofars:

אבינו שבשמים יתקדש שמך תבוא מלכותך יעשה רצונך
כבשמים כן בארץ את לחם חקנו תן לנו היום וסלח לנו
על חטאינו כפי שסולחים גם אנחנו לחוטאים לנו ואל
תביאנו לידי נסיון כי אם חלצנו מן הרע כי לך הממלכה
והגבורה והתפארת לעולמי עולמים אמן

We can also apply this concept in a cooperative worship with others. First, let me begin with CFTN. As mentioned earlier, my family and I partook in *Celebration 2023* in Wales. As soon as we arrived at the hotel in Wales where we stayed in 2013, I noticed a red lorry next to the entrance nearby the restaurant. Interestingly, the word 'Symphony' which was on the side of the red lorry caught my eye. I pondered immediately, 'Is this God's message?' Bearing this in my mind throughout *Celebration*, I tried to engage in praise and worship as much as I could.

This time the spiritual atmosphere was absolutely striking since *Celebration* had been resumed after a few years' gap due to COVID-19. Especially, it was the eighth *Celebration* for Wales. In numerology, number 8 is spiritually associated with harmony, balance, and abundance. It symbolises a new beginning after the seven days of God's creation and rest (שבת, Shabbat). Also, the number 8 signifies the deep connection to the spiritual realm because it represents the continuous flow of anointing between the physical and spiritual worlds. So, my expectation was quite high, thinking of 'Would the eighth

Celebration impact on me to deepen my spirituality?' Anyway the three words, 'symphony', 'harmony' and 'balance' took hold of me all the time during *Celebration 2023*.

As thinking of the encounter of the Samaritan woman at the well in Chapter 4 of John's Gospel, 'living water' mentioned in the conversation between Jesus and the woman is noteworthy. Jesus told her that He had come (to the world) to offer the living water which 'will become in them a spring of water welling up to eternal life' (John 4:14; NIV). He clearly saw the inner thirst of the woman which she was continually looking for even if her five partners for life couldn't satisfy. In the conversation Jesus mentioned of 'a time' when the true worshipers will worship the Father in the Spirit and in truth, and Father seeks this kind of worshipers because He is spirit.

Here Jesus mentioned 'the time' of the true worship will come to the worshipers. It implies that when the time comes, people can drink the living water while worshipping God. Perhaps I can elaborate this by sharing my personal experiences if you allow me.

During *Celebration 2023*, it was the day of the 12-hour worship if I am not mistaken. The spiritual atmosphere was intensified and saturated with the praise and worship throughout the day without ceasing. Around the late evening, my husband and I were blowing our shofars in due time -whenever the Spirit prompted us to do so. Thus, the ram's horn shofar was nearly almost in my left hand whereas my right hand was open wide. Strangely enough, I sort of felt the water passed through between my fingers as if I put my hand in a flowing stream. Immediately, I knew it was the 'living water' because I had such experience a couple of times before.

The first time I had was that many years ago my family and I partook in *Kingdom Foundations* (conference) hosted by *Global Awakening* in London. When the presence of the Holy Spirit was so thick, several people fell to the floor. Even when the meeting was over, people were still slain in the Spirit. As I walked around among them, I literally felt the living water up to my knees. It wasn't easy to walk around because of the heaviness of the water stream.

So, my experience of the living water for the second time during *Celebration 2023* was so precious and memorable. Apparently, this is what God has exactly promised to us through Gail Dixon, isn't it?

> *Gather the people together and I [God] will give them water. Then Israel sang this song: 'Spring up, O Well! All of you sing to it'* (Numbers 21:16-17).

Indeed, we all came together and sang together as He said. And then He responded with the 'living water' as He promised. Here is the power of a cooperative worship. This is a manifestation of His glory in a tangible way.

Not too long after *Celebration 2023*, I had a wonderful experience during a worship gathering at the local church in Peterborough where my family is currently with. As the host of the worship gathering on that Sunday morning began to declare the marvellous works of God one after another and then continued on for some time. Strangely enough, I sensed my inner spirit stayed tune to all his declarations and started to echo all one after another in unison. All of sudden, I felt a warmth on my right leg. As a matter of fact, prior to this Sunday gathering I was suffering from a sharp pain on my right foot and irritatingly had to hobble for a few days. Wow! To my surprise, the pain on my foot disappeared instantly. Yes, it happened as I harmonized with him in the worship gathering. Certainly, it was the power of the cooperative worship in harmony.

Now is the time for you to make a symphony for and before God. As you do, you will experience the 'living water' from Him and then it remains in you and wells up to eternal life until you will see Him face to face (John 4:14). You can experience the 'living water' in both your own place and in cooperative worship gatherings. I personally know a lady whose spiritual fountain springs up the 'living water.'

Some years ago when my family and I were invited to her housewarming meal after her house move, we had time to bless her place as a token of our gratitude. As we walked around and blew our shofars for every nook and cranny of the house, my spiritual eyes were open suddenly. I saw a beautiful small fountain, springing up the water and running down continuously. When I told her about it, she said that it was the exact spot where she spent most of the time, rejoicing in the presence of God.

Right! Let me close this chapter with an invitation from God:

*Come, all you who are thirsty,
come to the living water that will never run dry!*

Six

I SAW THE LORD

In the year that King Uzziah died, I saw the Lord, high and exalted, seated on a throne; and the train of his robe filled the temple. Above him were seraphim, each with six wings: With two wings they covered their faces, with two they covered their feet, and with two they were flying. And they were calling to one another:

> "Holy, holy, holy is the Lord Almighty; the whole earth is full of his glory."

At the sound of their voices the doorposts and thresholds shook and the temple was filled with smoke.

> "Woe to me!" I cried. "I am ruined! For I am a man of unclean lips, and I live among a people of unclean lips, and my eyes have seen the King, the Lord Almighty."
>
> - Isaiah 6:1-5; NIV -

In the year that King Uzziah died (740/739 BC), Isaiah experienced an extraordinary phenomenon. In a trance he saw the Lord seated on a throne of magnificent glory. It was extremely rare to have such a supernatural experience in the Old Testament era. Needless to say, it is also rare occurrences among the Pentecostals in modern times.

Isaiah was completely and utterly awestruck by the vision of the temple and seraphim angels in the heavenly realm. Thus, he cried out, 'Woe to me!' in fear.

Who is Isaiah? To our knowledge, he is the prophet. He is not mentioned anywhere outside the Bible. So from the narratives in chapters 6-8, 20 and 36-39, we understand that he seems to have had easy access to the royal court (chapter 7), and to be well informed about the affairs of state. It is generally assumed that he came from a family that would have been included in the ruling classes; whether he was related to the royal family in some way is possible although entirely unknown. Nonetheless, from the way he writes we can say that he was well educated in the best traditions of the time.

What a blessing for such intelligent man to have the extraordinary supernatural experience! On the contrary, I sadly saw many who were intelligent and well educated often missed such opportunity due to their arrogance. One thing I can ensure you is that he or she -whether he or she is rich or poor, young or old, well-educated or illiterate- must have 'I-saw-the-Lord' encounter once in his or her life time. It is a life transforming occurrence. It lays a foundation for an unshakable and unchangeable faith in the Lord, no matter what. I guarantee you that he or she will become radical by willingly giving up his or her life for the Lord. Blessed are the pure in heart, for they will see God (Matthew 5:8).

It is noteworthy that Isaiah had this powerful encounter in the year when King Uzziah died. Why is it so important to mention about that? The nation would be in a chaotic moment due to the death of the king. Hence, the people might be in a dreadful fear for the uncertain future. Furthermore, King Uzziah ruled for fifty-two years since he sat on the throne at the age of 16. According to 2 Kings 15:3, he was a king that did right in the eyes of the Lord. He was very successful because he was willing to be instructed by the prophet Zacharia. Moreover, God helped him against the Philistines and against the Meunites. So the nation was extremely prosperous during his reign. And then his heart puffed up due to pride. One day he walked into the temple to burn incense on the altar. In the Old Testament days, the high priest was meant to burn incense on the altar as a regular offering to the Lord (Exodus 50:7-8). Even the priest Azariah went after the king with other priests to stop him from burning incense and attracting the wrath of God. Nevertheless, King Uzziah was furious and would not relent until God struck him with leprosy (more likely an infectious skin disease).

Here the Isaiah's encounter of the Lord sitting on the throne happened in the year of king's death. It implies a significant spiritual lesson: as the pride dies, the glory of God manifests. As the Scripture says, God opposes the proud but gives grace to the humble.

Now it really intrigues us to examine more biblical characters who had 'I-saw-the-Lord' encounter, doesn't it? Let us get started from the Old Testament.

Abraham

Abraham, Father of nations, was born and grown up in Ur of the Chaldeans (modern *Tall al-Muqayyar*, Iraq approximately 10 miles/16 km west of the present bed of the Euphrates River). His whole family set out from Ur to go to Canaan, but when they came to Harran, they settled there. Apparently, Abraham never knew Yahweh God until he reached the age of 75. What happened at the time? When his father Terah died in Harran, God called him for the first time. Genesis 12 narrates it as below:

> The Lord had *said to* Abram, 'Go from your country, your people and your father's household to the land I will show you. I will make you into a great nation, and I will bless you; I will make your name great, and you will be a blessing. I will bless those who bless you, and whoever curses you I will curse; and all peoples on earth will be blessed through you.' So Abram *went*, as the Lord had told him (*Italics mine*, Genesis 12:1-4a; NIV).

For Abraham it definitely was a remarkable encounter of Yahweh God. Can you imagine that Abraham heard His voice? Absurdly, he simply left by faith as God had said to him because he had just heard His voice. Does it make sense to you? Was he stupid or crazy? Perhaps he was or wasn't. I can assure you that what he experienced was extremely rare so that he couldn't resist it.

Again, sometime later the word of God came to Abram in a vision (Genesis 15:1). We can see God made a covenant with Abraham in a trance, '... as the sun was setting, Abram fell into a deep sleep' (Genesis 15:12; NIV). At the age of 100 Abraham had a miracle baby as God had promised. 'Shall a child be born to a man who is one hundred years old?' was Abraham's thought when the promised was given to him one year earlier. The more repeatedly he experienced God and His miracle, the stronger he could trust in Him after all. As we are aware of it, by faith he willingly gave up his precious son, Isaac as a burnt offering to God when He tested him later on.

ða

Moses

Moses led the Jews from slavery in Egypt, known as the *Exodus*. The Lord called him from the burning bush in the mountain of God, *Horeb*. For the first time, Moses heard the voice of Yahweh, God of Abraham, of Isaac and of Jacob who he had only heard about but never experienced before. What was his immediate response afterwards? He hid his face in fear (Exodus 3:6). Needless to say, this encounter changed his entire life and made him a heroic leader of the Israelite by carrying out God's divine mission for the Jews later on.

Truly, Moses had an intimate relationship with God who spoke to him face to face, as one speaks to a friend (Exodus 33:11; Numbers 12:8). When he asked God to show him His glory, he was placed in the cleft of the rock, and then God came in glory and covered him with His hand until His glory passed by so that he wouldn't die in His presence. Moses was the very unique human being who experienced God's glory by seeing His back (Exodus 33:18-23). Even his face was radiant while having an intensive and intimate time with God for 40 days and 40 nights on the mountain so all the people of Israel were afraid to come near him (Exodus 34:29-35).

Samuel

The encounter of Samuel, the last of the ruling judges in the Old Testament, was quite unique. Samuel served the Lord by assisting Eli, the priest. Around that time, messages from the Lord were very rare, and also visions were quite uncommon (1 Samuel 3:1).

One night Eli had gone to bed. The lamp of God had not yet gone out, and Samuel was sleeping in the Tabernacle near the Ark of God. All of sudden, the Lord called out, 'Samuel!' Samuel didn't know the Lord, meaning no personal relationship with God, and then ran to Eli. Eli said, 'I didn't call, son. Lie down.' This repeated three times and at last Samuel began to hear His voice. As we know, he became a hearer and an intercessor for the people of Israel and a messenger of God during his life time.

David

David, the king of Israel, was once a shepherd for his father Jesse, a man of Bethlehem. He was the youngest of eight sons and became the family shepherd according to the custom around the time. It is generally understood that the Arab peasant is a shepherd as well as a farmer of grain. So as the older son grows up, he transfers his role from sheep caring to helping the father with sowing, ploughing, and harvesting the crops, and passes on the shepherd's task to the next younger boy. Thus, the job is passed from older to younger until the youngest of all becomes the family shepherd. This explains why we can see features of sheep, pastures and shepherd in many of David's Psalms.

As a matter of fact, Psalms are Hebrew religious hymns/praises. Unquestionably, many of the Psalms were composed by David. The well-known Psalm 23 portrays God as a good shepherd, feeding and leading His flock. The rod and staff are also the implements of a shepherd. God as the care taker leads the sheep to green pastures and still waters because He knows that each of His sheep must be personally led to be fed. David as being a caretaker of the sheep was well trained by God to be a heroic warrior and good shepherd for His people later on. We can see it clearly when he was about to confront the giant Goliath as 1 Samuel 17:34-36 (NIV) recounts it:

David said to Saul, 'Your servant has been keeping his father's sheep. When a lion or a bear came and carried off a sheep from the flock, I went after it, struck it and rescued the sheep from its mouth. When it turned on me, I seized it by its hair, struck it and killed it. Your servant has killed both the lion and the bear.'

Imagine what David could do while shepherding his father's sheep in the wilderness. I believe that whenever he would find time, he would praise and worship God with an ancient Hebrew lyre (kinnor). How often did he praise and worship God? I assumed he did it all the time. The Hungarian composer and pianist Franz Liszt once said, 'If I miss practicing one day, I know it; if I miss two days, my friends know it; and if I miss three days, the public knows it.' As we know, he was a very skilful player to have been chosen for King Saul who was mentally suffering and being tormented by the evil spirit.

Now the Spirit of the Lord departed from Saul, and a harmful spirit from the Lord tormented him. And Saul's servants said to him, 'Behold now, a harmful spirit from God is tormenting you. Let our lord now command your servants who are before you to seek out *a man who is skillful in playing the lyre*, and when the harmful spirit from God is upon you, he will play it, and you will be well.' So Saul said to his servants, 'Provide for me a man who can play well and bring him to me.' One of the young men answered, 'Behold, I have seen a son of Jesse the Bethlehemite, *who is skillful in playing*, a man of valour, a man of war, prudent in speech, and a man of good presence, and the Lord is with him.' Therefore Saul sent messengers to Jesse and said, 'Send me David your son, who is with the sheep.' And Jesse took a donkey laden with bread and a skin of wine and a young goat and sent them by David his son to Saul. And David came to Saul and entered his service. And Saul loved him greatly, and he became his armour-bearer. And Saul sent to Jesse, saying, 'Let David remain in my service, for he has found favour in my sight.' And whenever the harmful spirit from God was upon Saul, David took the lyre and played it with his hand. So Saul was refreshed and was well, and *the harmful spirit departed from him.* (*Italics mine*; 1 Samuel 16:14-23; ESV)

From 1 Samuel 16 above, there is no doubt that David was a spirit-filled and anointed player. His anointed music drove out the evil spirit from Saul because the spirit of the Lord was there, so was freedom (2 Corinthians 3:17b).

ે**&**

Paul

The Damascus road experience is arguably the most important event in the life of Paul, the apostle. This remarkable account is repeatedly recorded several times in Acts (9:1-9; 22:6-11 and 26:12-18) and in Paul's own letters (1 Corinthians 15:3-8; Galatians 1:11-16). As a passionate Pharisee, he persecuted the early Church believers and was travelling on the road to Damascus in order to persecute the Jewish Christians there. On this trip he powerfully encountered the resurrected Jesus.

> About noon as I came near Damascus, suddenly a bright light from heaven flashed around me. I fell to the ground and heard a voice say to me, 'Saul! Saul! Why do you persecute me?' 'Who are you, Lord?' I asked. 'I am Jesus of Nazareth, whom you are persecuting,' he replied. My companions saw the light, but they did not understand the voice of him who was speaking to me. 'What shall I do, Lord?' I asked. 'Get up,' the Lord said, 'and go into Damascus. There you will be told all that you have been assigned to do.' My companions led me by the hand into Damascus, because the brilliance of the light had blinded me (Acts 22:6-11; NIV).

This powerful encounter happened because God chose him to be an instrument to proclaim Jesus to the Gentiles and their kings and to the people of Israel (Acts 9:15). Throughout the book of Acts (especially after chapter 13) we can see what Paul had gone through: hard labour, imprisonments, beatings and frequent threats of death. He said, 'Five times I received at the hands of the Jews the forty lashes less one. Three times I was beaten with rods. Once I was stoned. Three times I was shipwrecked; a night and a day I was adrift at sea' (2 Corinthians 11:24-25; ESV).

What amazing testimonies these are! What made all the people above become radical and sincerely kept their faith until the moment of their death? There is no doubt that they personally encountered God and acknowledged that they were sojourners on earth but would return to a heavenly place where God had prepared for them (Hebrews 11:13-16). So, they ran the race set before them patiently and finished the line triumphantly.

Seven

WHY JESUS?

The greatest blessing I have is 'knowing Jesus' (Y'shua ישוע in Hebrew). The Hebrew verb form of knowing is 'yada' (ידע). It includes an intimate relationship between a man and a woman of a married couple. So, when I say 'knowing Jesus' here, it is more likely to 'yada' in a deeper sense.

'Knowing Jesus' can begin with understanding what His name means. The meaning of the Hebrew name *Y'shua* is 'salvation,' taken from the verb *yasha* (ישע) which means 'to deliver, save, or rescue.' As mentioned earlier, people's name determines their destiny very much. Thus, God changed their names into new ones for fulfillment of their destiny. In this respect, one thing for sure is that Jesus came to the world for 'salvation' as His name means. This can raise several questions, 'whom did he save?', 'from whom or what did he deliver?', 'why the world needs to be rescued?', 'how did he deliver?' etc. In a nut shell, humanity fell into sin by eating the forbidden fruit in the Garden of Eden. Hence, we become slaves of (inherited) sin (like genes). In order to be free from the slavery, the price must be paid. Jesus' sacrifice (blood) became the means of atonement for sin, that is, the reconciliation between God and humans was made by His atoning sacrifice. Sin requires punishment. In order to avoid punishment, in the Old Testament animal sacrifices as a substitute were made to cover the penalty of the sin.

Again, we raise questions, 'why did Jesus come to the world as a human being?' or 'could He choose a different way to deal with the sin issue?' or 'was becoming a human the only way for Him to deal with the sin issue?' Truly omnipotent God could do anything or/and any way to save the world, couldn't He?' Then why did He choose to be a human being, *incarnation*?

First of all, we need to carefully think about 'how the sin issue must be dealt with.'

From the book of Genesis, we understand that animals were sacrificed to cover the sin of Adam and Eve. 'The Lord God made garments of skin for Adam and his wife and clothed them' (Genesis 3:21; NIV). As a matter of fact, the man-made leafy coverings were not appropriate to cover their guilt and shame, therefore, God instead made leather coverings for them. It implies that the sin issue won't be resolved without shedding blood. Surely, the animal sacrifice was God's method of forgiveness for sins of mankind. Actually, when an animal sacrifice was offered to God in the Old Testament, a male bull or sheep or goat without defect should have been given. Why? The reason is that the sin(s) was transferred from the offeror to the animal by laying hands on the head of the offering. Therefore, in this regard the offering animal must be pure and blameless.

One day an intelligent gentleman challenged me with a question, 'why does Christianity executively insist that Jesus is the only way while others with different/diverse religious backgrounds do good works?' Have you ever thought of this or a similar question before? The following is my answer to the question.

'Religion' is a man-made belief system towards supernatural beings whereas Christianity is not a religion but *'relationship'* with divine deity (God). Christianity is totally different because the deity first came to the humanity whereas the former doesn't. That is why a Christian faith only begins with an individual relationship with God whereas other religions claim that good works or merits of humanity lead to salvation. In other words, when he or she confesses that God is real and willingly has a relationship with him through the work of Jesus (on behalf of us) done on the cross, then his or her faith journey begins. Why should God be the only one (not other supernatural beings) to have a relationship? It can be understood from Genesis 15.

God *first* came to Abraham in a vision and made a covenant with him.

> He [God] said to him, 'Bring me a heifer three years old, a female goat three years old, a ram three years old, a turtledove, and a young pigeon.' And he brought him all these, cut them

> in half, and laid each half over against the other. But he did not cut the birds in half. (Genesis 15:9-10; ESV)

Generally speaking, making a covenant means two or more parties come together to make a contract, agreeing on promises, stipulations, privileges, and responsibilities. Here 'a covenant relationship' between God and Abraham in the Hebraic way (cutting animals in half) was made. This ritual covenant is similar to a marriage ceremony. From the moment that you would make a marriage vow, you would be obliged to be faithful to your spouse only for the rest of your married life. It is the same with God. He hates adultery, i.e., loving Him as well as loving idols (syncretism). Therefore, God must be the only one whom we must relate to.

Let us closely look at 'why did Jesus come to the world and die as a human being?' Especially, take a note that He came as a baby who was utterly vulnerable (not in a glorious king appearance). That is why many Jews still wait for the Messiah whom they can imagine and think of. Yet, Apostle John describes, 'the Word [Jesus] became flesh and made his dwelling among us' (John 1:14; NIV). Then again we can raise a question, 'why did Jesus become a human?' The simple answer is 'to be like us.'

> Since the children have flesh and blood, he too *shared in their humanity* so that by his death he might break the power of him who holds the power of death -that is, the devil- and free those who all their lives were held in

slavery by their fear of death. (*Italics mine*; Hebrews 2:14-15; NIV)

Jesus did so with several reasons: first of all, He would destroy the work of the devil. Secondly, He could snatch the keys of death and Hades (Revelation 1:18) so that He set us free from fear of dying. Thirdly, He could serve as a faithful chief priest in God's presence. Fourthly, He made peace with God for our sins (Hebrews 2:17). Fifthly, He experienced temptation when He suffered, thus He is able to help us when we are tempted (Hebrews 2:18). Sixthly, He took upon Himself our suffering and carried our sorrows; He was wounded for our rebellious acts; He was crushed for our sins (Isaiah 53:4-5). Seventhly, He became the first fruits of the resurrection so that we know that we will be resurrected like Him (1 Corinthians 15:20-23). Lastly, He demonstrated how *to love God and love our neighbours*. '…the Son of Man did not come to be served, but to serve' (Matthew 20:28a; NIV).

Now this leads to another question, 'why then did He choose a crucifixion death?'

In history, crucifixion was frequently used as a method of capital punishment for political or religious agitators, pirates, slaves, and the worst of criminals by the Persians, Carthaginians and Romans, among others. The victim was tied and/or nailed to a crossbeam and left to hang until death. According to accounts of crucifixion, it was one of the most disgraceful and painful forms of death, and also one of the most dreaded methods of execution in the ancient world. Especially, the nails were typically made of iron, measured between 5 and 7 inches in length, and the act of hammering them into the flesh would have been excruciatingly painful. In addition to the physical pain, the psychological and emotional trauma of being publicly executed in such a manner cannot be overstated. Despite such painful and terrible death process, Jesus had to be crucified. Why? 'Christ redeemed us from the curse of the law by becoming a curse for us - for it is written, cursed is everyone who is hanged on a tree' (Galatians 3:13; NIV) He took our curses on the tree and died with the curses in order to set us free.

Wait! Jesus' death is not the end. It is much more exciting to know what happened after He died. Come with me to explore it!

According to Luke 23:43, '... truly I tell you [thief on the cross], today you will be with me in *paradise*' (*Italics mine*), Jesus went to *paradise*. 'Paradise' is generally understood as a place of blessing where the righteous go after death whereas the wicked go to hell/Hades. In the Hebraic view, 'sheol' is a subterranean underworld where both the righteous and the unrighteous dead go: the upper level of 'sheol' (paradise) for the righteous and the lower level (Hades) for the unrighteous. For right now, let us say that paradise and hell or 'sheol' are temporary holding places until the day when Jesus comes back to judge the world based on whether individuals have believed in Him or not.

1 Peter 3:18-20 (ESV; *Italics mine*) says, 'Christ also suffered once for sins, the righteous for the unrighteous, that he might bring us to God, being put to death in the flesh but made alive in the spirit, in which he went and *proclaimed to the spirits in prison* because they formerly did not obey, when God's patience waited in the days of

Noah, while the ark was being prepared.' From the scriptures above, Jesus went to 'sheol' and made an announcement to the dead spirits imprisoned there. How could He do so? Jesus was also a human being; therefore, He was able to go there because He died like other human beings. Yet, He straightforwardly confronted death and Hades and then snatched the keys from both of them. So, we no longer fear death because the new owner of the keys is Jesus.

Eight

CATCH ME UP IN YOUR STORY, LORD

Would you be surprised if I say that you can be a co-author of God's story which He is writing? It means that you can be a history maker. Yes, you can become the history maker if you are willing to go for it.

As you see yourself, do you wonder how *little ol' me* can be the history maker? No worries. You can be the one if you are in the hand of the Master, *your Creator*.

Do you remember the story of Jesus' feeding thousands with **the boy's** meal -five pieces of barley bread and two small fish? Presumably, there were more than five thousand people (plus many women and children) although all four Gospel books describe it as a miracle of feeding of the 5,000. I often wondered that the boy was not the only one who had food at that time. Why then did others not offer theirs? The five pieces of the bread and two fish are just humble food from a poor family as we can expect. Perhaps some of them might think that their food was not good; others would think that theirs were not much so that they couldn't share them with others, etc. There must be various and reasonable pretexts of not offering their food. Here the boy who was simple (and perhaps inspired by Jesus' teaching) gave his all to Him. Imagine when his food was in the hand of Jesus, the miracle broke out! If you were in his shoes, you were really thrilled, weren't you? The boy must be very excited and delighted because he had witnessed multiplication with his own eyes, especially, it happened with his humble meal. Who could expect such an amazing miracle? It was only possible because of the sacrifice and trust that the boy made at the time.

In the Gospels, there are **two women** who washed Jesus' feet with their hair: *Mary* (the sister of Lazarus and Martha) and *an unnamed prostitute*. Some critics of the Gospels argue that the writers recorded the same event but Luke's account clearly shows that they are different occasions. One took place at the home of the leper Simon in Bethany (Mark 14:3) whereas the other took place at the house of a Pharisee Simon in Galilee (Luke 7:36). I assume that one could influence the other so that we can see the similar events happened in the Gospels. Nevertheless, what they did for Jesus is still remembered by all Bible believers around the world because of their sacrifice and love for him.

The very first chapter of the book of Matthew begins with the genealogy of Jesus. Honestly speaking, many of us feel bored to read this part. Nevertheless, we shouldn't miss its importance with a couple of reasons. First of all, for centuries in various cultures, one's genealogy has been a source of political and social status. Secondly, it is generally recorded by men's names from generation to next generation. Thus, it is noteworthy that there are five women in Jesus' genealogy: Tamar, Rahab, Ruth, Bathsheba (Uriah's wife), and Mary (Jesus' mother). We shouldn't miss to find out *who they are* because they appeared in the king's genealogy. Let us begin with Tamar.

The book of Genesis narrates that **Tamar**, the daughter of Shem, the son of Noah became Judah's daughter-in-law. When Judah's firstborn Er died, Judah gave her his second son, Onan as a surrogate for his dead brother who would beget a son to continue Er's lineage. Onan, however, refused to do this by spilling his semen on the ground. For this behaviour, God killed him on the spot. Judah was afraid to give his youngest son, Shelah to Tamar. As a result, Judah wronged her. While she was waiting for Shelah to grow up and marry her, she realised that her father-in-law did not intend that union. So, she planned to secure her own future by deceiving her father-in-law to sleep with her. She covered herself with a veil so that Judah wouldn't recognize her, and then she sat in the roadway at the entrance to Enaim. Judah propositions her, offering to give her a kid for her services and giving her his seal and staff in pledge. Then Tamar was pregnant, and Judah commanded to burn her. However, she sent back his pledge to him to prove her innocence. Judah publicly announced her innocence, saying that 'she is more in the right than I' (Gen 38:26; NIV). She gave birth to twins, Perez and Zerah. She secured her place in the Judah's family line with her loyalty and sincerity.

The main characteristics of **Rahab** described in the Bible are a harlot, a Canaanite, and a liar. Her story is found in the book of Joshua. Joshua sent out two spies to examine the fighting force of Jericho while the Israelites were camping at Shittim in the Jordan valley across from Jericho. Rahab hid the spies by covering them with bundles of flax on the roof. She said to the spies after protecting them from capture:

> I know that the Lord has given you this land and that a great fear of you has fallen on us, so that all who live in this country are melting in fear because of you. We have heard how the Lord dried up the water of the Red Sea for you when you came out of Egypt and what you did to Sihon and Og, the two kings of the Amorites east of the Jordan, whom you completely destroyed. When we heard of it, our hearts melted in fear and everyone's courage failed because of you, for the Lord your God is God in heaven above and on the earth below. "Now then, please swear to me by the Lord that you will show kindness to my family, because I have shown kindness to you. Give me a sure sign that you will spare the lives of my father and mother, my brothers and sisters, and all who belong to them -and that you will save us from death (Joshua 2:9-13; NIV).

When Jericho fell, Rahab and her whole family were saved from the agreement of the spies and then were included among the Jewish people. She became mother of Boaz, great-grandfather of King David. Despite her status (gentile and harlot), she secured her place in the Jesus' family line by faith (Hebrews 11:31).

Ruth's story begins with Naomi, an Israelite woman and her husband, Elimelech who left their hometown Bethlehem due to the famine at the time. They settled in the nearby nation of Moab. Eventually, Elimelech died and her two sons married Moabite women named Orpah and Ruth. After ten years of marriage, both of Naomi's sons died, too. Naomi decided to return to her homeland since the famine subsided and had no longer immediate family in Moab. She told her daughters-in-law about her plan, and both of them said they would go with her. Nevertheless, Naomi encouraged them to stay in their homeland and to start new lives. Orpah eventually agreed but Ruth insisted, 'Where you go I will go, and where you stay I will stay. Your people will be my people and your God my God' (Ruth 1:16b; NIV).

Both Naomi and Ruth arrived in Israel while the barley harvest was underway. They were poor so that Ruth had to go out to glean food that fell on the ground while harvesters were gathering the crops. The field Ruth was working in belonged to Boaz who was a relative of Naomi's late husband. With Naomi's advice, Ruth asked Boaz to act as a kinsman redeemer, and Boaz married her. Ruth gave birth to a son named Obed who was the grandfather of King David. Ruth demonstrated her loyalty to the Jewish family and willingly obeyed her mother-in-law. In the end, she secured her place in Jesus' bloodline.

According to the Jewish custom, the Book of Ruth is read during Shavuot (the Feast of Week) to celebrate the giving of the Torah to the Jewish people. The reason is that Ruth's story took place during the spring harvest, which is when *Shavuot* falls.

The first time **Bathsheba**'s name is mentioned in 2 Samuel 11:3. King David sent his messengers to find out about her when he saw her bathe from the roof of the palace. Don't judge her by saying 'why did she have a bath in his sight? Did she intentionally do so to seduce him?' I don't want to argue with you but ensure you that she just finished her monthly cycle and performed ceremonial cleansing according to the Law of Moses.

Anyway, David found out that she was the daughter of Eliam and the wife of Uriah who were his mighty (thirty-seven) warriors (2 Samuel 23:8-39). Her husband was away at war at the time.

Now bad things happened to her one after another. First, she was forcefully taken to the palace and slept with King David. Remember she lived in a time when women were looked upon as property. Furthermore, she had no right to resist the King' demand/order. Otherwise she would not be sent back home safely without having sex with him. Second, she became pregnant afterwards and had to inform him about it, likely in a panic. Third, she was told her husband had died not long after this. Unfortunately, she became a pregnant widow. Fourth, her newborn baby died just seven days after the prophet Nathan rebuked King David (2 Samuel 12:1-23).

After all this turmoil, God eventually redeemed her life. Here is God's grace. He gave her the wisest son, Solomon. Thus, she became the king's mother and secured her place in the genealogy of Jesus after all. This is Bathsheba who was a woman who endured much suffering and overcame.

Mary, the mother of Jesus is found in the Gospels and in the book of Acts. Mary's story begins with angel Gabriel's visit to announce the most incredible news that she would have a child, and her son would be the Messiah for the world. Mary's calling held great honor, yet, it would cost great suffering and a disgrace as an unwed mother in a society which the adulteress must be sentenced to death by stoning. Mary was young, poor, and female from Nazareth in Galilee which seemed to be unfit for the great calling from God in the eyes of her people. On the contrary, God saw her trust and obedience so that He could fulfill His wonderful plan for the whole of humanity. Her willingness to sacrifice everything for God's plan came out of love and trust. So, she submitted her life to God no matter what it would cost her. Apparently, her determination, obedience and faith secured her place in the genealogy of Jesus.

Jochebed is the mother of Moses. Her story is found in chapter two of Exodus, Exodus 6:20, and Numbers 26:59. And it goes like this.

Many years had passed since the death of Joseph. Although Joseph had saved the country from a great famine, he was forgotten by the Pharaohs as time passed. In the beginning chapter of Exodus it says the Pharaoh was afraid of the Jews because they were many and would join a foreign army against the Egyptians. Thus, he ordered all male Hebrew babies to be killed. When Jochebed bore a son, she hid him for three months. Instead of letting him be murdered, she took a basket, coated by tar and put the baby in it. She set it among the reeds on the bank of the Nile River. Then Pharaoh's daughter came to have a bath in the river. One of her maidservants saw the basket and brought it to her. The baby's sister Miriam watched to see what would happen. With courage she asked Pharaoh's daughter if she could get a Hebrew woman to nurse the child. She was told to do that. Miriam fetched her mother, Jochebed and brought her back. Jochebed nursed her own son until he grew. Then she took him to Pharaoh's daughter, who raised him as her own and named him Moses. Later on Moses was used by God as His servant to bring the Hebrew people out from slavery to the edge of the Promised Land.

Jochebed was a woman of faith and honoured God by keeping His commandment - not murdering the baby. She feared God more than she did the Pharaoh. Therefore, she saved Moses without knowing that God would use him for His great plan. Doubtlessly, she became a history maker because of her trust and fear of the Lord.

Do you know who Haddassah is? She is a beautiful young queen whose Babylonian name is **Esther**. She lived in ancient Persia after the Babylonian captivity. When her parents died, her older cousin Mordecai adopted and raised her. After the king of the Persian Empire, Xerxes I deposed Queen Vashti, he hosted a royal beauty pageant to find his new wife. Esther was chosen for the throne.

At the time the king's highest official Haman hated the Jews, especially Mordecai who had refused to bow down to him. He planned a wicked plot to annihilate all the Jews on a specific day. Mordecai found out the plot and shared it with Esther and challenged her to plead with the king for mercy upon the Jews. Esther urged all of the Jews to fast and pray for deliverance and mercy. After that, she risked her own life and boldly approached the king with a request. She invited both the king and Haman to a banquet where eventually she revealed her Jewish heritage to the king as well as Haman's plot to have her and her people killed. In a rage, the king ordered Haman to be hung on the gallows -the very same gallows he had built for Mordecai. The end of Esther's story is happy: Mordecai was promoted to Haman's high position, and the Jews were granted protection throughout the whole land. Hence, the Jews celebrated God's deliverance, and the festival of Purim was instituted afterwards.

Who could imagine an orphan and a foreigner to be enthroned? Esther's characteristics made her a historic figure. First, she was obedient so she took Mordecai's words and saved her people in danger. Second, she was pious so she fasted and prepared spiritually by praying to the heavenly king before pleading to the earthly king. Third, she was wise so she provided banquets to soften the king's heart first although she was graciously allowed to make her supplication to him immediately when he had extended his golden scepter to her. Fourth, she was a woman of great compassion. Even though it put her in great danger, she courageously went to the king and pleaded for the lives of the Jews.

Esther is one of the outstanding women of faith in the Bible. Her beauty pairs well with her obedience, faith, courage, wisdom, and decisiveness which made her a history maker.

Gideon is known as the greatest judge of Israel

although he was from the least of the least in terms of tribes. His story is found in Judges 6:11.

The angel of the Lord appeared in Ophrah that belonged to Gideon's father Joash the Abiezrite. At the time Gideon was threshing wheat in a winepress to keep it from the Midianites. What? Was the greatest judge of Israel threshing wheat in a winepress? Furthermore, surprisingly the angel said to him, 'The Lord is with you, mighty warrior.' He looked cowardly, didn't he? Interestingly, God regarded him as a mighty warrior. And then God called him to deliver His suffering people from the Midianites who depleted Israel's supplies. Gideon didn't believe it at first when he was told that he would save the people of Israel from the enemy. So he tested God using fleece. First, he required God to put dew on a fleece that he had laid out on the ground, ending up with a wet fleece and dry ground. Then he asked God for the opposite - a dry fleece and wet ground. After this Gideon could totally rely on him. For instance, God told him to reduce the number of the army from 32,000 to 300 men who would fight against the Midianites. And he did so. God then received the glory as the 300 men brought a victory according to His strategy.

Gideon was a simple and ordinary man, yet became a mighty warrior as God saw. What we should take a note here is that he was obedient and absolutely trusted God. Certainly, God saw these characteristics and his potential to be a mighty warrior.

Boaz was a wealthy man from the clan of Elimelek and also was mentioned in the genealogy of Jesus. He was Ruth's husband and a great-grandfather of King David.

As we saw earlier, Boaz appeared in the book of Ruth when she worked in his field as a gleaner after settling down in Bethlehem. Boaz had already heard of Ruth's loving care for Naomi and spoke to her, assuring her that she would be provided for in his field. And then he secretly told his harvesters to leave behind some stalks of grain so that she would have gathered more. That evening, when Ruth's mother-in-law Naomi found out that Ruth had been working in Boaz's field, she identified him as a close kinsman-redeemer who had the privilege to act on behalf of a relative in need. As taking Naomi's advice, Ruth went to Boaz to let him know that she needed a kinsman-redeemer. Boaz told Ruth that he was pleased to offer her redemption, which would include marriage to her, but there was one relative who was closer in line to be the kinsman-redeemer. The next day, Boaz met with the other relative and presented the situation that Naomi and Ruth faced. The man declined to marry Ruth, and Boaz then made a commitment in front of the town's leaders that he would take Ruth as his wife. Then Boaz and Ruth were married, and Obed was born afterwards.

Indeed, it is a beautiful love story of a man and a woman. Despite his wealth, he had still been a single man at his (relatively) old age until he met Ruth. We might think because he was born of a Jewish father and a Gentile mother. Moreover, his mother Rahab was a harlot before the fall of Jericho as we saw earlier. The Bible doesn't tell us more about him, thus we conclude that it might be God's plan to bless him because of his characteristics. First, he was generous and thoughtful as we see how he treated Naomi and Ruth with care. Second, he trusted God in the process of decision-making. Although he was not the first candidate of being kinsman-redeemer, he surrendered everything to God's hand. So, God blessed him with a baby boy as a result. By faith Boaz became a history maker.

Daniel's three friends **Shadrach, Meshach** and **Abed-Nego** (or their Hebrew names Hananiah, Mishael and Azariah) served as advisers to King Nebuchadnezzar of Babylon. The three and Daniel were taken from their homes in Jerusalem (605 B.C.) during a siege by King Nebuchadnezzar of Babylon. All four were intelligent, good-looking young men at the time of their capture, and they were likely of the royal family or nobility of Judah. Then the king instructed the chief of his eunuchs, Ashpenaz to train some of the Jewish children for three years in order to serve in the king's palace afterwards. The three and Daniel were selected by Ashpenaz for the three-year training. And they were taught the language and literature of the Chaldeans (Daniel 1:3-4).

One night Nebuchadnezzar had a troubling dream so he called all his magicians, enchanters, sorcerers, and astrologers. He demanded them to tell him what dream he had and its interpretation. Since they failed in providing an answer, Nebuchadnezzar was greatly furious and ordered the execution of all the wise men of Babylon. Now the three and Daniel were also classified as wise men after the training, so they faced the same judgement. With wisdom Daniel was able to handle the situation properly. He asked King Nebuchadnezzar for time so that he might interpret the dream for him.

After that Daniel urged the three to plead for mercy from God concerning this mystery so that they might not be executed with the rest of the wise men of

Babylon. During the night the mystery was revealed to Daniel in a vision.

When confronting the king, Daniel indicated the dream was prophetic and concerned the political dominance that Gentiles would exercise in the future. He continued to say that the dream was of a very huge statue with a head of gold, chest and arms of silver, belly and thighs of bronze, legs of iron, and feet of iron mixed with baked clay. Eventually, this statue was struck on the feet by a rock, which made it crumble and blow away. The rock then grew into a mountain that filled the earth (Daniel 2:31-35).

Daniel explained that the head of gold was Nebuchadnezzar himself, who ruled the Babylon worldwide empire, but that would end in the future giving rise to two inferior nations which would rule for a time. Then again there would be more power changes, with each ruling nation or nations less competent than the ones before. Eventually, a new leader, represented by the striking stone would bring them all to an end, and he would then rule forever.

With this incident Daniel was promoted into a high position with many gifts awarded. On top of it, the king made him ruler over the entire province of Babylon and placed him in charge of all its wise men. At Daniel's request the king also appointed Shadrach, Meshach and Abednego administrators over the province of Babylon.

Time passed. King Nebuchadnezzar decided to erect a magnificent gold statue according to his image expecting everyone to respect and worship it. On the day of the statue's dedication ceremony on the plains of Dura outside of Babylon, everyone was instructed that they must bow down before the statue and worship it. When all were gathered, a herald proclaimed, 'Nations and peoples of every language, this is what you are commanded to do: As soon as you hear the sound of the horn, flute, zither, lyre, harp, pipe and all kinds of music, you must fall down and worship the image of gold that King Nebuchadnezzar has set up. Whoever does not fall down and worship will immediately be thrown into a blazing furnace' (Daniel 3:4-6; NIV). Yet, Shadrach, Meshach, and Abednego decided to defy this command.

Some officials brought accusation upon the three. The king became furious with them but graciously gave them another chance to avoid such punishment. 'Is it true, Shadrach, Meshach and Abednego, that you do not serve my gods or worship the image of gold I have set up? Now when you hear the sound of the horn, flute, zither, lyre, harp, pipe and all kinds of music, if you are ready to fall down and worship the image I made, very good. But if you do not worship it, you will be thrown immediately into a blazing furnace. Then what god will be able to rescue you from my hand?' (Daniel 3:14-15; NIV)

The three determined not to worship the image, saying, 'King Nebuchadnezzar, we do not need to defend ourselves before you in this matter. If we are thrown into the blazing furnace, the God we serve is able to deliver us from it, and he will deliver us from Your Majesty's hand. But even if he does not, we want you to know, Your Majesty, that we will not serve your gods or worship the image of gold you have set up' (Daniel 3:16-18; NIV).

Being found guilty by law, the three were bound and

thrown in the blazing fire. The king was extremely angry and instructed that the fire should be increased seven times more than customary, even the soldiers that brought them to the furnace were burnt.

While King Nebuchadnezzar was observing this event from a safe distance, he noticed the unbound men walking around inside the flames with the three. Then the king leaped to his feet in amazement and asked his advisers 'Weren't there three men that we tied up and threw into the fire?' and shouted 'I see four men walking around in the fire, unbound and unharmed, and the fourth looks like a son of the gods' (Daniel 3:24-25; NIV).

The king immediately recognised that the Lord of the three is truly God, and he commanded them to come out from the furnace. Neither their bodies, nor their hair, nor their clothes were burnt. By now he knew that the Lord was superior to his Babylonian gods, and he blessed them and honoured them by decreeing that the Lord was to be honoured. Furthermore, he graciously promoted them to higher positions with greater power in his kingdom.

The unshakable faith of the three is remarkable and enabled the pagan king to acknowledge the Lord as the supreme God above all gods. Their astute, faithful and steadfast characteristics made them history makers.

Phinehas was the son of Eleazar and grandson of Aaron, the first High Priest of Israel. Numbers 25 describes what he did.

With the counsel of Balaam, who encouraged the Midianite women to seduce the men of Israel, Israel plunged into sexual immorality and idolatry (Numbers 25:1-3). One of the Israelite leaders took a Midianite woman into a tent nearby the Tabernacle 'in the sight of Moses and in the sight of the whole congregation of the people of Israel' (Numbers 25:6; ESV). Previously, the foreign influence of the Midianite woman only occurred *outside* the Israelite camp as they 'invited the people to the sacrifices of their gods' (Numbers 25:2; ESV). Now the defiant act of the Israelite leader who took a Midianites woman *inside* the Israelite camp showed that the corruption was beginning to completely overtake the people.

Phinehas then took a spear and killed both the Israelite man and the Midianite woman. As a result, the plague which the Lord had brought upon the people as a judgment ceased (Numbers 25:8). As the Lord accepted the acts of Phinehas for atonement on Israel's behalf, He suspended His wrath against the Israelites. He also secured Phinehas' place in the Levitical Priesthood (Numbers 25:10-13). Indeed, a list of his descendants who served in this position is given in the book of Chronicles. Most famous among them is Ezra the scribe and priest who was a Jewish leader at the beginning of the Second Temple period.

Nehemiah was a Jewish cupbearer to a pagan king named Artaxerxes, who reigned from the city of Susa (modern day's Iran).

The story of Nehemiah begins with a dreadful report from those who had lately been in the ruined Jerusalem: its walls were broken and their gates were on fire. Nehemiah was full of remorse and cried out to God for mercy. As a cupbearer he acquired the king's favour and was able to go to Jerusalem with king's letters -giving him safe journey and resources from the king's forest (Nehemiah 2:1-10).

Nehemiah was involved in rebuilding the broken walls in Jerusalem. He surveyed it himself first and spoke to the people about the plan to rebuild it. When some evil people came to oppose the work, he didn't abandon it but remained focused on rebuilding the walls. After completing the walls, he continued to do what was right in the sight of God. He gathered the people and listed them according to genealogy (Nehemiah 7). And then he had God's word read to them by Ezra the priest (Nehemiah 8).

Along with Ezra the priest, Nehemiah worked to bring people back to the Lord:

> And Nehemiah, who was the governor, Ezra the priest and scribe, and the Levites who taught the people said to all the people, 'this day is holy to the Lord your God; do not mourn nor weep.' For all the people wept, when they heard the words of the Law (Nehemiah 8:9; ESV).

Also, he was compassionate and fought against the oppression among the Jews. So, he commanded other officials and nobles to forgive outstanding debts and return lands acquired through taxes to the people (Nehemiah 5:1-13).

Despite being governor, he didn't take an advantage of

the provisions allotted for him. Unlike previous governors who burdened the people, he didn't because of the fear of God (Nehemiah 5:15). He did not place a heavy burden on the people, either. Nehemiah feared the Lord so he did not abuse his authority. Rather, he used his position to bring people to the Lord.

Another important thing to pay attention to is that he was a man of prayer. When the king asked him what he requested of him, his first response was to pray to God immediately (Nehemiah 2:4).

Certainly, we can tell what characteristics of his made him a history maker. First, he was prayerful when he was told about the dreadful situation of Jerusalem. In chapter 1 he spent a long time in prayer from the heart. Also, he quickly prayed to God before making the request to the earthly king.

Second, he believed God would use him to get the wall rebuilt. Thus, he never tried to attack his enemies but sincerely trusted God who would deal with them when the opposition arose.

Third, he acted with wisdom and planned things carefully. For instance, when the king asked how he could help, he took the letters signed by the king and picked up the supplies along the journey. Once he arrived in Jerusalem, he waited three days without announcing his presence. He then secretly inspected the damage of the city at night.

Fourth, he as a leader spoke to all the people and inspired them to work together. He organised workers for the various sections of the wall and dealt with any challenge raised. He also fed 150 Jews and officials daily without using his allowance as governor.

Fifth, he was a man of integrity not only for the heavenly king but also the earthly king. For instance, he kept his promise to return to King Artaxerxes and then returned to Jerusalem again (Nehemiah 13:6). When he discovered that some leaders had let an evil enemy have a room in the courts of the Lord, he threw them out and restored the workers in the house of God. He stopped people from working and selling on the Sabbath, and commended the Levites to purify themselves and perform their duties (Nehemiah 13:8-22 and 30).

Judah, the fourth Son of Jacob and Leah, was the father of the family as a royal line which Messiah would come from. The name originated in Leah's words of praise to the Lord on account of his birth: 'This time I will praise the Lord. Therefore she named him Judah' (Genesis 29:35b; NASB).

Jacob's favorite wife, Rachel had a son, Joseph, who became his most beloved child. This provoked his elder brothers to jealousy. So, they plotted to kill him and threw him into a pit. When an Ishmaelite caravan passed by, Judah suggested selling Joseph rather than killing him.

Judah moved away from the clan and married the daughter of a man named Shua, with whom he had three sons: Eir, Onan, and Selah. Eir married a woman named Tamar, who then married Onan after Eir died. When Onan died, Judah was slow to allow her to marry his third son. Nevertheless, Tamar deceived Judah and became pregnant with the twin boys as we have seen earlier.

When famine hit Canaan, Jacob sent his older sons to Egypt to purchase food -not knowing that the high-ranking Egyptian official they were dealing with was actually Joseph. He did not send Rachel's second son Benjamin, fearing that he would be harmed. They eventually ran out of food and needed to return to Egypt, but Jacob refused to send Benjamin until Judah took personal responsibility for his safe return.

Joseph framed his brother, Benjamin by putting a silver goblet in his grain sack as a pretext for detaining him in Egypt. Judah bravely stood up to him, risking his life to save his little brother, coming full circle from how he had treated Joseph many years earlier.

Before Jacob died, he blessed each of his sons. On Judah's turn, he compared his son to a young lion and declared that 'the scepter will not depart from Judah' (Genesis 49:10a; NIV). Apparently, kings like David and Solomon came out from his descendants.

Judah received the most favorable treatment in Genesis among Jacob's sons (other than Joseph). According to biblical historians it is a reflection on the historical primacy that the tribe of Judah possessed throughout much of Israel's history including the line of David.

Joseph, a son of Jacob and Rachel, was favoured by his father who gave him a coloured coat and sold by his half-brothers to Egypt. When Joseph arrived in Egypt, he was eventually sold to Potiphar, one of Pharaoh's officials.

Potiphar's wife was attracted by his handsome looks and desired to sleep with him. One day, when no one was home other than the two of them, she grasped Joseph's garment and demanded him to sleep with her. Joseph slid out of his cloak and ran outside to avoid the temptation. And then she turned the tables on Joseph, telling her husband that it was Joseph who had enticed her. As a result, Potiphar was furious and put him in prison.

Time passed. Pharaoh dreamed two dreams, which none of his advisors were able to interpret. The cupbearer, who once was in prison and remembered the Hebrew youth from his prison days, suggested that Joseph be summoned. Joseph interpreted Pharaoh's dreams as being a divine prediction for seven years of plenty followed by seven years of famine, and advised Pharaoh to prepare by storing grain during the first seven years. Impressed by Joseph's wisdom, Pharaoh made him as the second ruler and tasked him with preparing the nation for the seven years of famine.

Meanwhile, the famine also affected Canaan. Hearing that there was grain in Egypt, Joseph's brothers journeyed there to buy food. Joseph decided to use this opportunity to find out whether his brothers truly regretted having sold him. Joseph tested his brothers' determination to save their youngest brother Benjamin -Joseph's only maternal brother- from the plot he set up for him. Once he saw their genuine attitude towards Benjamin, Joseph finally revealed his identity to his siblings.

Following the family reunion in Egypt, Joseph's father and his family settled in Goshen. This entire event served as the backdrop for Israel's ultimate enslavement in Egypt and the subsequent Exodus later on as God said to Abraham, 'Know for certain that for four hundred years your descendants will be strangers in a country not their own and that they will be enslaved and mistreated there' (Genesis 15:13: NIV).

God raised up Joseph, the dreamer for his ultimate goal - *Exodus!* It is God's deliverance of Israel from slavery to make them a great nation. Joseph was greatly used by God in that sense, yet we shouldn't forget that he had to suffer many things in his life time. However, he was faithful, and his integrity and fear of the Lord proved that he was qualified to be a history maker.

There is another man called **Joseph** in the Bible. He was chosen by God to be Jesus' earthly father. The Gospel of Matthew tells us that he was a righteous man. His actions towards his betrothed Mary showed that he was a kind and sensitive man.

When he was told that she was pregnant, he had every right to feel not only confused, but also disgraced since he knew the child was not his own so that Mary's unfaithfulness could carry a social stigma. Based on Jewish law, he had the right to divorce Mary and put her to death by stoning. On the contrary, his initial reaction was to break off the engagement, and he treated Mary with extreme kindness and respect. Even he didn't want to cause her further shame, so he decided to do it quietly.

In the midst God sent an angel to Joseph to reassure him that his marriage to her was His will. Joseph willingly obeyed God regardless of the public humiliation he would face. This shows his character and faith. Surely,

God honored Joseph's integrity by entrusting him with a great responsibility.

According to Luke's account, he was not rich and mainly earned the income through his carpentry job. When the time came for the purification according to the Law of Moses, Jesus was presented at the temple with 'a pair of turtledoves or two young pigeons' which was concession for someone who could not afford a lamb as a sacrifice. God deliberately chose Joseph to bring up Jesus in a humble environment so that Jesus had 'no stately form or majesty' to attract people from an earthly viewpoint (Isaiah 53:2b).

Joseph was chosen to be a history maker as Jesus' earthly father because of his integrity, obedience and faithfulness.

Nicodemus was a leading Pharisee and well-known religious leader of the Jewish people. He was also a member of the Sanhedrin, the Supreme Court in ancient Israel.

He came to Jesus secretively at night with a question since he acknowledged that God must have sent Jesus because of all the miraculous signs He performed. Jesus got to the heart of the matter by the truth: '… no one can see the kingdom of God unless they are born again' (John 3:3; NIV).

Nicodemus then asked Jesus how anyone can be born twice. Jesus taught him about the need to be born of the Spirit. Then Nicodemus simply asked, 'How can this be?' (John 3:9). For this, Jesus explained to him with an

Old Testament story which a Pharisee should have known. 'Just as Moses lifted up the snake in the wilderness, so the Son of Man must be lifted up, that everyone who believes may have eternal life in him' (John 3:14-15; NIV). In the context of his conversation, one of the most famous biblical passages, John 3:16, occurs:

> For God so loved the world that he gave his
> only Son, so that everyone who believes in him
> may not perish but may have eternal life.

After this encounter, we may not truly know what has changed in Nicodemus' life but can assume that he became a follower of Jesus. Here is one of the accounts.

When some of the chief priests and Pharisees of the Sanhedrin asked why the temple guards failed to bring Jesus to them, Nicodemus spoke to them in defense of Jesus, saying that Jewish law requires that a person cannot be condemned without first being heard (John 7:50-51).

Another account is that after Jesus' crucifixion, Nicodemus and Joseph of Arimathea laid his body in a nearby tomb together at great risk to his safety and reputation. He prepared a proper burial by bringing a mixture of expensive myrrh and aloes (about 75 pounds) to embalm him according to John's Gospel. This amount of spice was enough to fittingly bury royalty, signalling that Nicodemus had recognized Jesus as King.

As a chief tax collector for the vicinity of Jericho, **Zacchaeus** worked for the Roman Empire although he was a Jew. Under the Roman system, tax collectors pledged to raise a certain amount of money, and anything they could raise over that amount was their personal profit. As the Gospel of Luke says, he was a wealthy man so he must have extorted a great deal from the people and encouraged his colleagues to do the same.

Jesus was passing through Jericho one day. Zacchaeus was excited to hear that He was visiting the town. He was curious and eager to see Him despite his short stature by climbing a sycamore tree because he could not see Him over the crowd. To his surprise, Jesus stopped, looked up, and said, 'Zacchaeus, come down immediately. I must stay at your house today' (Luke 19:5; NIV).

At Zacchaeus' home, Jesus told the parable of the ten servants. Moved by Jesus' message, Zacchaeus promised to give half his money to the poor and repay fourfold anyone he had cheated. Jesus told him that salvation would come to his house that day. Zacchaeus is not mentioned again in the Bible after that episode. Nonetheless, we can assume his repentant spirit and his acceptance of Jesus led to his salvation and the salvation of his whole household.

This is a perfect example of Jesus' earthly mission to seek and bring salvation to the lost even tax collectors like Zacchaeus who were corrupt and despised as traitors since they solely worked for the Roman Empire.

Interestingly, the name Zacchaeus in Hebrew means 'pure' or 'innocent.' Certainly, as a tax collector, he didn't live up to his name. On top of it, the characteristics of

Zacchaeus -a rich tax collector and short stature and cannot see Jesus- made him difficult to be saved or to have access to Jesus. Despite all these, he became a history maker because of his willingness to see Jesus and acceptance by faith.

As we have seen so far, there are a great cloud of examples in the Bible although I have simply chosen some of them here regardless of whether they are young or old, men or women, rich or poor, well-known or anonymous, significant or insignificant, godly or ungodly in the past, etc. Common quality or characteristics of these people which made them history makers are 'simplicity of faith.' When the opportunity of becoming a history maker came to them, they simply accepted it by faith without doubt. Perhaps they might be the ones who God looked for. 'God looks down from heaven on all mankind to see if there are any who understand, any who seek God' (Psalm 53:2; NIV).

Alright! I would like to close this chapter by inviting you to join the history maker cloud. Why not allow the Lord to catch you up in His story? If any sin which hinders you to do so, ask Him to forgive you first. By a simple gesture of your surrender to Him you can be a history maker.

> Let us throw off everything that hinders and the sin that so easily entangles. And let us run with perseverance the race marked out for us, fixing our eyes on Jesus, the pioneer and perfecter of faith. For the joy set before him he endured the cross, scorning its shame, and sat down at the right hand of the throne of God. Consider him who endured such opposition from sinners, so

that you will not grow weary and lose heart.
(Hebrews 12: 1-3; NIV)

EPILOGUE

There was one day that I heard the voice of the Lord, saying, 'Whom shall I call to do My work?' Then I said, 'Here am I, Lord.' And then He said, 'Go and tell people about My work.' Then I said, 'So be it.'

• • •

When young Mary, the mother of Jesus encountered the angel, Gabriel, she was told that she will be with a child who will be the Saviour of the world later on. What was her response? When the boy with the five loaves of the bread and two fish was told that the twelve disciples were looking for food to be fed, what was his response? While Miriam, the sister of Moses was watching and noticing that the Pharaoh's daughter fetched her baby brother from the Nile River, what was her immediate response? When Queen Esther was told that she should plead the king for saving the whole Jews which might put her at risk, what was her response? When the governor Nehemiah heard the terrible news of the ruined wall and burnt gates in Jerusalem, what was his response? One common denominator they had was *willingness* to do the Lord's plan.

As recalling the moment that the Lord prompted me to

do this book project, I was quite excited about it. With a simple faith, I willingly agreed to do so. I first thought that it won't be difficult because I am happy to write, nevertheless, it turned out to be a challenge to go through. To be frank, I was almost tempted to abort the book project as soon as I faced an objection, long delay, and procrastination. With God's intervention I changed my mind, thinking, 'Can I abort a baby because I'm struggling with all these uneasiness at the moment? Can I have a joy without great sacrifice made from bearing a life and bringing it out to the world in due time? If I don't do this, what legacy will the next generation have when I am gone? For their sake, I shouldn't give up.' Then a scripture related to His nature popped up before my eye was Isaiah 55:11 (NIV), 'so is my word that goes out from my mouth: It will not return to me empty, but will accomplish what I desire and achieve the purpose for which I sent it.' This is it! If He does it, and He achieves it, then what else can I say? So, my prayer was 'Lord, please give me wisdom and more perseverance to complete the mission.'

In the beginning of writing the book, I was not sure of what should be recorded. And then it came to a point that it could be an anthology of *Celebration* stories from others who have been together over the years. All of us have something special to talk about from different perspectives and can learn from each other. Furthermore, God seemed to urge me metaphorically that we can write together this time just like a symphony form in music.

As mentioned earlier, we partook in *Celebration 2023*. Therefore, I had to stop writing for a while and went to Wales for a week. Do you remember what word I saw when we arrived at the hotel? It was 'Symphony' on the side of the red lorry. Certainly, His message was loud and clear. Anyway, I was assured that there was no doubt that it should be a 'symphony' book. However, I never knew that it was going to be a huge challenge because we worked differently at our own pace. Now, I humbly say that I am glad to have a chance in order to learn 'how to work together well' in the process of the project. Here I can clearly see a beauty of the 'symphony' afterwards.

Moreover, another occasion strongly convinced me that the book should be written, no matter what. There was a baptism ceremony of 12 people at church not too long ago. One of their testimonies encouraged me saying, 'It's worth it!' The testimony goes like this.

A young lady came back to her faith because of her grandmother's journal. After her passing, she saw her journal and read it. The journal was filled with godly devotion and prayers for her grandmother's loved ones. All the written words pointed to Jesus. I can imagine that her grandmother didn't see her granddaughter came back to the Lord while she was here on earth. Nonetheless, she faithfully wrote about what she believed and prayed for them sincerely. Yea, I can write and compile what God wants both others and me to record up to this point and to pass on to the next generation just like what the grandmother did.

At the end of the interview with the Harris couple in Wales, Colin mentioned about a song[8] from the 1970s

---

[8] Ronnie Wilson's *I Hear the Sound of Rustling*. (1979); Kingsway's Thankyou Music

which is a very timely word for the moment. So, I have quoted its refrain here:

> *My tongue will be the pen of a ready writer and what the Father gives to me I'll sing; I only want to be His breath, I only want to glory the King.*

In the beginning of the first CFTN, none of us truly knew where it was heading and what it would be onwards, yet one thing was so sure: we carried on every summer year after year at various places of different countries.

Now I can see the children of CFTN who were born over the past years become young adults at the time of writing. I imagine that the main runner of CFTN is going to shift to the next generation. I dream that this book may become one of their treasured possessions to cherish and remember what our generation has done so far. Also, I dream that they will use our spiritual legacy as a springboard to unleash their anointing and even take them to the next level on their spiritual journey. Here I am delighted to close the book with the triad of my song, my prayer and my blessing for the generation to come.

My song for the next generation

This morning my time with the Lord began with a song titled, *Raise A Hallelujah*. Many in a Christian circle know the testimony behind this song.

A gifted and anointed couple of musicians, Jonathan and Melissa Helser wrote it as a powerful declaration over the life of their friends' son, Jaxon whose kidney got infected by E.coli virus. Boy Jaxon had to have blood transfusions and go on dialysis afterwards. Jaxon's parents asked their church community to pray for him.

A few days before Christmas, Jonathan received a text message from his friends, Joel and Janie Taylor, saying that Jaxon was in a critical condition, and they didn't think the child would make it.

As soon as Jonathan got that text, he felt like the giant of unbelief stood in front of him. He thought Jaxon was going to die that night. Then, something indescribable happened to him and his wife. While they were praying for a miracle, all of sudden a song came out of their mouths which they began to sing a powerful declaration against the giant that Jaxon was facing. Certainly, the song became a powerful weapon against the giant enemy. With medical treatment and countless prayers, a God's miracle was granted to the Taylors. Jaxon became well.

Indeed, there is great power behind praise and worship when we lift up our God high and glorify Him. By the way, 'Hallelujah' is a transliteration of Hebrew, הללו (hallu) + יה (yah) which means 'Praise Yah!' The word *hallel* in Hebrew means a joyous praise in song. The second part, 'Yah' is a shortened form of YHWH. So raising a Hallelujah means 'to raise a joyous song to God,' no matter what. That explains why bringing out the Hallelujah in us is so powerful to destroy the enemy.

In the book of Acts (Chapter 16), we can see two men named Paul and Silas who were followers of Jesus and passionately shared the good news of salvation with the Gentiles. One day on their mission, they encountered a young slave girl who practised a spirit of divination while going into the place of prayer in Philippi, a major city of Macedonia and a Roman colony. She earned a lot of money for her masters by telling fortunes. This girl followed Paul and Silas around and was making a lot of noise, proclaiming that they were servants of the Most High God. Her repeated words were true, but Paul became annoyed and cast out the evil spirit from her. This angered her owners who profited from her ability. Thus, the owners seized both Paul and Silas and brought them before the authorities, falsely accusing them of causing disturbances in the city. Then the magistrates ordered them to be severely beaten and thrown into prison afterwards.

In the depths of their suffering, Paul and Silas began to sing hymns and praise God while confined in the inner dungeon. Their worship at midnight had a profound impact not only on their own lives but also on those around them. Imagine that as they worshiped, the other prisoners listened. Surely, their worship resonated in the hearts of those who heard them. Of course, they knew nothing about the worship and its power which could set them free from their physical and spiritual bondage.

Suddenly, there was a massive earthquake, and the prison started to shake its foundations. All the doors immediately flew open, and the chains of every prisoner fell off! The jailer woke up and saw the prison doors wide open. He assumed the prisoners had escaped, so he drew his sword to kill himself. At the moment, Paul shouted at him not to kill himself. The jailer called for lights and ran to the dungeon and fell down trembling before Paul and Silas. And then he brought them out and asked, 'Sirs, what must I do to be saved?' Not only the jailer but also his entire household were saved because of this incident.

The story of Paul and Silas reminds us of the great importance of praise and worship during difficult times. Certainly, it shows the power of worship and praise. Also, there was a mighty power of freedom in worship and praise, breaking the chains and opening the prison doors!

At the time of writing, the news outlet is busy to report on Israel-Gaza war every day. The war broke out on Shabbat day (Saturday) when Hamas and Islamic Jihad fired thousands of rockets from Gaza early in the morning and armed Palestinian militants broke down the hi-tech barriers surrounding the strip to enter Israel, shooting and taking hostages. On Sunday after Hamas' attack, the Israeli prime minister declared and warned Israelis to face a long and difficult war. I don't know what they are exactly fighting each other for although it is said that it is a land conflict between the two superficially and a precondition for the prophetic fulfilment of Ezekiel 38 biblically, nor do I know how long the war will go on; yet, timely, I apprehend another war from my daily reading, 2 Chronicles 20, this morning.

The Moabites and Ammonites with some of the Meunites came to wage war against Jehoshaphat, the fourth king of the kingdom of Judah.

For this, the people of Judah from every town in Judah and the king gathered together to seek help from the Lord. All the men of Judah, with their wives and children and little ones, stood there before the Lord. And then King Jehoshaphat stood up in the assembly at Jerusalem and prayed at the temple of the Lord in the front of the new courtyard. Afterwards the words of the Lord delivered to them through Jahaziel, a Levite and descendant of Asaph:

> Do not be afraid or discouraged because of this vast army. For the battle is not yours, but God's. Tomorrow march down against them. They will be climbing up by the Pass of Ziz, and you will find them at the end of the gorge in the Desert of Jeruel. You will not have to fight this battle. Take up your positions; stand firm and see the deliverance the Lord will give you, Judah and Jerusalem. Do not be afraid; do not be discouraged. Go out to face them tomorrow, and the Lord will be with you (2 Chronicles 20:16-17; NIV).

And then all the people of Judah and Jerusalem put down their heads in worship, and the Levites praised the Lord in loud voices. The following morning, they left for the Desert of Tekoa. As they were to set out, King Jehoshaphat encouraged the people to have faith in God and also trust in the prophets of God. And then he appointed some singers to **praise God at the head of the army**. The rest of the scriptures are very interesting to read.

God fought for the Israelites and then made them collect the plunder of the enemy for three days:

> As they began to sing and praise, the Lord set ambushes against the men of Ammon and Moab and Mount Seir who were invading Judah, and they were defeated. The Ammonites and Moabites rose up against the men from Mount Seir to destroy and annihilate them. After they finished slaughtering the men from Seir, they helped to destroy one another. When the men of Judah came to the place that overlooks the desert and looked toward the vast army, they saw only dead bodies lying on the ground; no one had escaped. So Jehoshaphat and his men went to carry off their plunder, and they found among them a great amount of equipment and clothing and also articles of value -more than they could take away. There was so much plunder that it took three days to collect it. On the fourth day they assembled in the Valley of Berakah, where they praised the Lord. This is why it is called the Valley of Berakah to this day. Then, led by Jehoshaphat, all the men of Judah and Jerusalem returned joyfully to Jerusalem, for the Lord had given them cause to rejoice over their enemies. They entered Jerusalem and went to the temple of the Lord with harps and lyres and trumpets. The fear of God came on all the surrounding kingdoms when they heard

how the Lord had fought against the enemies of Israel (2 Chronicles 20:21-29; NIV).

Again, we can see the powerful weapon of the war: *praise and worship in faith*. Whether we are facing the battle physically and/or spiritually, we should remember that it absolutely belongs to Him, no matter what and when. Here I declare the sovereignty of God over the Israeli-Hamas war at present, and lift up my praises to Him. I release the anthem of triumph in advance because God has already won the battle.

I do remember what Pastor Bill Johnson at Bethel Church mentioned on *Understanding Principles for Spiritual Warfare*. When we offer our spirit, soul, and body to glorify God's name, something happens: the air becomes charged with the power of God's presence because He shows up in that moment to deliver us. In this respect, giving thanks to God and praising Him is solely to celebrate what He has done and who He is. We are just stepping onto His altar by saying, 'Here I am. Do as You please, Lord. Accomplish Your purposes in this situation and over the matter.'

Now, I am dreaming of the generation to arise who will raise their Hallelujahs. Doubtlessly, the kingdom of God will invade the earth and individual life with the great power of the Hallelujahs. Yes, here I gladly release this song for the generation to come:

Whom shall I send?
And who will go for Us?
Do you hear it?
Don't cover your ears.
Do you hear His heartbeat for you?
Don't turn your back.
Do you hear His passionate calling?
Don't go far away from Him.
Don't go.
He is your loving Father, patiently
waiting for you to come.
He is waiting.
Now is the time to come to His love.
Now is the time to draw closer to His heart.
Let a Hallelujah arise within you.
Let your Hallelujah be a weapon for His kingdom.
Arise!
Arise!
Arise!

My prayer for the next generation

Chapter 17 of the Gospel John narrates the prayer of Jesus before he was arrested. He prayed for His disciples and all believers.

On memorial occasions, I often pray the same prayer because it always gives me tears, and also I can feel His heart whenever I prayed with it. Let us think this for a moment. What would the very last prayer of yours be before going to the home in heaven? Certainly, Jesus' prayer has everything that I can think of. With the same heart, I would like to pray for the generation to come.

> *Father in heaven, I bring the next generation before You. I thank You and believe that You have a great and immeasurable plan for them to fulfil for the sake of You and Your kingdom. I bless Your holy name for them. I believe that Your name will be glorified through the new generation to come. Father, grant them authority over all people so that many will come to Your kingdom through them and have eternal life to be with You forever. Would you show them who You have created them to be? Let them hear Your voice and let them find the greatest value in You. Father, teach them to know You in depth and have experiential knowledge of You day by day so that they will flourish and grow in a deep sense of belonging in You. Let their heart open to Your will. Father, let the generation courageously arise for Your kingdom. Fill them continuously with Your Spirit and let them know the power of intercession so that their prayer knees are always in Your presence. Give them boldness and wisdom to overcome all evil. Let young troops come to the battle for You like morning dews as I saw them on 'Festival Fields' in Wales. Father, be a mighty shield for them and continue to make Yourself known to them*

and sanctify them by Your truth. Let the generation be marked and sealed by You. Father, I lovingly commit them in Your hand in Jesus' name. Amen.

My blessing for the next generation

To bless young ones is a beautiful Jewish tradition. In the Old Testament, Jacob was the one who knew the importance of his father's blessing for the firstborn son and deceived Isaac his father to steal the blessing even he wasn't the firstborn son. Surely, later on he called all his twelve sons for a final blessing before his death. Thus, Jacob's blessing becomes an example to the Jewish people for all time.

Apparently, in the Torah, blessings are seen as a channel for spiritual and physical potential. Remember in the beginning God himself blessed Adam and Eve to multiply and fill the world. Also, remember there is power of words from our mouth. 'Death and life are in the power of the tongue' (Proverbs 18:21a; ESV). God created all things with His words, didn't He? Even people know that a curse has power to impact on their/others life badly. Numbers 22:4-6 (ESV) exactly shows that Balaam was hired to curse the people of Israel.

> So Balak the son of Zippor, who was king of Moab at that time, sent messengers to Balaam the son of Beor at Pethor, which is near the River in the land of the people of Amaw, to call him, saying, "Behold, a people has come out of Egypt. They cover the face of the earth, and they are dwelling opposite me. Come now, curse this people for me, since they are too mighty for me. Perhaps I shall be able to defeat them and drive them from the land, for I know that he whom you bless is blessed, and he whom you curse is cursed."

Roy Godwin, who is the executive director of *Ffald-y-Brenin Trust*, a Missional House of Prayer and Christian Retreat Center in Wales and the author of *I Will Bless Them*, says that all believers can be God's conduits for blessing to those around us. The reason is that God has given us (believers) the authority and the command to bless others in order to release the manifest presence of God into our world. Especially, he mentioned that there is a difference in blessing others in Jesus' name and shared a remarkable story of a Chinese community blessed by one man. The story goes like this.

> *Years ago somebody sent me a newsletter from another nation which tells the story of a Chinese community. It was an extraordinary area within China that was well renowned and famous for many things that spoke a blessing. The crops*

were always amazing; there were no divorces; there was no violence; there was no alcoholism. It had become a big tourist area because the air itself seems so healthy. Everybody slept so well and so peacefully. Then suddenly everything went wrong. There were big conversations about how that could happen. Interestingly, what they discovered was that there was an elderly man who used to climb the hill every sunset and every sunrise. He was a Christian and would lift his hands to the Lord and turned slowly 360 degrees speaking blessings in Jesus' name over every household and every community and over the land in that area. It was a fairly lone hill in a very flat area so that he could see so much of it. He was just speaking out blessings in Jesus' name. He was a lone Christian in that whole area. When he died, speaking blessing stopped and then the place deteriorated. As people realised that, they called for a Christian in a nearby city to come and explain what that meant. Somebody came and told them about Jesus. The person said that God blessed us by sending his son Jesus and explained 'what blessing was about' and 'who Jesus was' and 'how they could come to know Him and the eternal life' and 'how to bless in the way that elderly person had blessed to bring transformation.' This is a fairy tale ending to that story because they just said 'yes' and then there was a wonderful restoration in that community again.

Apparently, Roy began to learn so much about 'a spoken blessing in the name of Jesus which led to fruit of transformation since then.

To conclude, I would also love to bless the next generation with the Aaronic/priestly Blessing, recorded in Numbers 6:23-27. It is the blessing that Aaron and his sons were to speak over the people of Israel. It expresses the highest state of blessing that the nation would enjoy as they obey the word of God and are continuously faithful to Him. According to Numbers 6:27 (ESV; *Italics mine*), after the Aaronic priests recited this blessing over the people, God declared, 'So shall they put my name upon the people of Israel, and I will *bless them*.' I truly believe His word: when I bless the next generation, then He will bless them.

Here I will do it in the same manner as I always do for my family at home and others elsewhere. In the name of Jesus I speak this over you, *the next generation*:

The Lord bless you;
The Lord keep you;
The Lord make His face shine upon you;
The Lord be gracious to you;
The Lord lift up His countenance upon you
and favour you;
The Lord establish shalom(peace) in you.

Our stories end here but your story continues ...

ABOUT THE AUTHOR

Hana has lived in various countries and was involved in several missions in the past. She has a husband and a 15 year-old daughter. She studied in a wide range of academic disciplines in Pharmacy, Healing Ministry, Missiology, Christian Counselling, English Language Teaching, Linguistics, and Applied Linguistics in (Learner Training and Language Testing). She and her family participated in *Celebration For The Nations* in Wales (2007-2014 and 2023) and in Israel (2016-2017), and founded and ran *Celebration Colchester* for two years until they went to Mozambique to be part of 'Harvest School' (*Iris Global*) in June-October, 2015. From 2016 her husband and she are the co-founders of *Nehemiah 9.3 Mission* (www.nehemiah93.com). She currently works on the second series of *Shofar-blowing*.

Printed in Great Britain
by Amazon